EYEWITNESS
FOSSIL

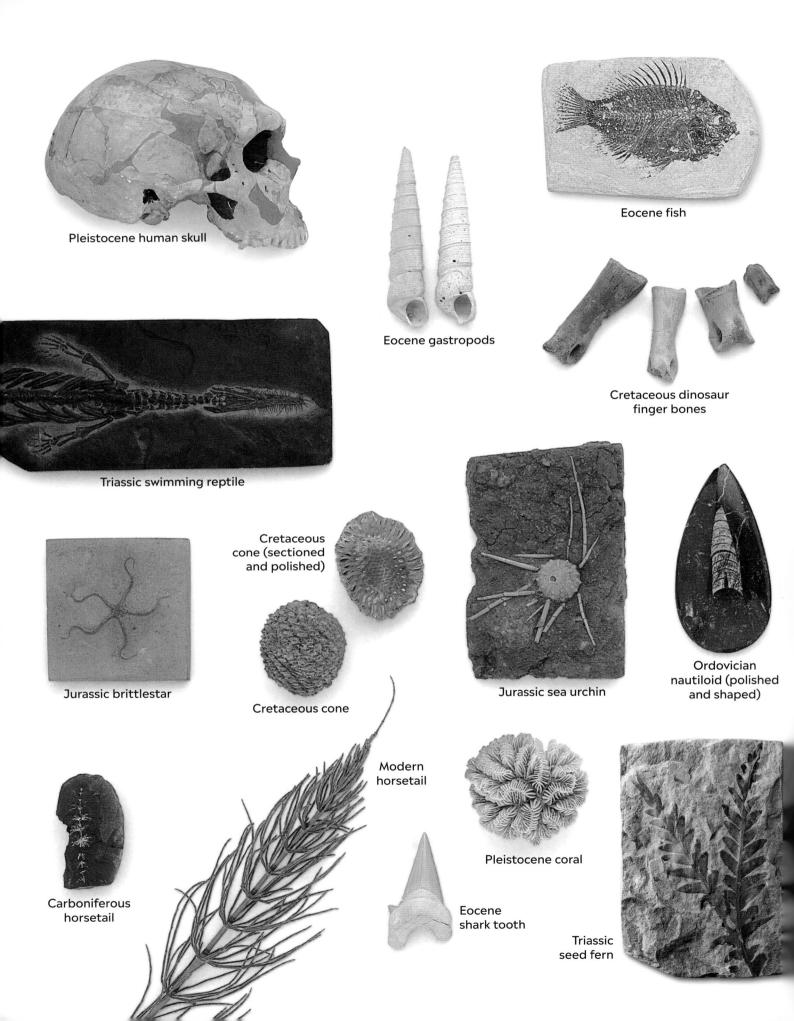

Pleistocene human skull

Eocene gastropods

Eocene fish

Cretaceous dinosaur finger bones

Triassic swimming reptile

Jurassic brittlestar

Cretaceous cone (sectioned and polished)

Cretaceous cone

Jurassic sea urchin

Ordovician nautiloid (polished and shaped)

Carboniferous horsetail

Modern horsetail

Pleistocene coral

Eocene shark tooth

Triassic seed fern

Jurassic ammonite
(carved as a
snakestone)

EYEWITNESS
FOSSIL

Written by
DR. PAUL D. TAYLOR

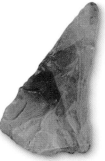

Pleistocene
hand ax

Carboniferous
lycopod

Eocene fish

Silurian
brachiopod

Permian tree fern
(sectioned and polished)

Pliocene
scallop

Modern coral

Triassic
dinosaur
footprint

DK

Pleistocene coral

Cretaceous dinosaur tooth

Jurassic ammonite

Cretaceous bryozoan

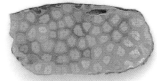

Jurassic coral (sectioned and polished)

Cretaceous opalized gastropod

19th-century microscope for examining thin sections

Carboniferous spider

Cretaceous opalized bivalve

Pleistocene sea urchin

Cretaceous worm tube

Miocene corals

Pleistocene gastropods

Silurian sea lily

Miocene bat jaws

Modern magnolia flower

DK | Penguin Random House

REVISED EDITION

DK DELHI

Senior Editor Virien Chopra **Senior Art Editor** Vikas Chauhan
Assistant Editor Zarak Rais **Art Editor** Tanvi Sahu
Assistant Art Editor Prateek Maurya **Assistant Picture Researcher** Nunhoih Guite
Managing Editor Kingshuk Ghoshal **Managing Art Editor** Govind Mittal
DTP Designers Pawan Kumar, Vikram Singh, Deepak Mittal
Jackets Designer Vidushi Chaudhry
Senior Jackets Coordinator Priyanka Sharma Saddi

DK LONDON

Senior Editors Michelle Crane, Jenny Sich **Senior Art Editor** Sheila Collins
US Senior Editor Jennette ElNaggar **US Executive Editor** Lori Cates Hand
Managing Editor Francesca Baines **Managing Art Editor** Philip Letsu
Production Editor Gillian Reid **Production Controller** Jack Matts
Senior Jackets Designer Surabhi Wadhwa-Gandhi
Jacket Design Development Manager Sophia MTT
Publisher Andrew Macintyre **Associate Publishing Director** Liz Wheeler
Art Director Karen Self **Publishing Director** Jonathan Metcalf

Consultant Dr. Paul D. Taylor

FIRST EDITION

DK LONDON

Project Editor Louise Pritchard **Art Editor** Alison Anholt-White
Senior Editor Sophie Mitchell **Senior Art Editor** Julia Harris
Editorial Director Sue Unstead **Art Director** Anne-Marie Bulat
Special photography Colin Keates (Natural History Museum, London)

PAPERBACK EDITION

Managing Editors Linda Esposito, Andrew Macintyre
Managing Art Editor Jane Thomas **Category Publisher** Linda Martin
Art Director Simon Webb **Editor and reference compiler** Clare Hibbert
Art Editor Joanna Pocock **Production** Jenny Jacoby
Picture Research Celia Dearing **DTP Designer** Siu Yin Ho
Consultant Kim Bryan

This Eyewitness ® Guide has been conceived by
Dorling Kindersley Limited and Editions Gallimard

This American Edition, 2023
First American Edition, 1990
Published in the United States by DK Publishing
1745 Broadway, 20th Floor, New York, NY 10019

Copyright © 1990, 2003, 2017, 2023 Dorling Kindersley Limited
DK, a Division of Penguin Random House LLC
24 25 26 27 10 9 8 7 6 5 4 3 2
002-338858-Dec/2023

A catalog record for this book is available from the Library of Congress.
ISBN 978-0-7440-9206-6 (Paperback)
ISBN 978-0-7440-9207-3 (ALB)

DK books are available at special discounts when purchased in bulk
for sales promotions, premiums, fund-raising, or educational use.
For details, contact: DK Publishing Special Markets,
1745 Broadway, 20th Floor, New York, NY 10019
SpecialSales@dk.com

Printed and bound in China

www.dk.com

MIX
Paper from responsible sources
FSC™ C018179

This book was made with Forest
Stewardship Council™ certified
paper—one small step in DK's
commitment to a sustainable future.
For more information go to
www.dk.com/our-green-pledge

Slide of thin section of Carboniferous bryozoans

Jurassic ammonites

Silurian trilobite (mounted as a brooch)

Contents

Fossils—true and false

Fossils are the remains or evidence of animals or plants that have been preserved naturally. They range from the skeletons of huge dinosaurs to tiny plants and animals. Most fossils are formed from the hard parts of animals and plants, such as shells, bones, teeth, or wood. Footprints, eggs, and burrows can be fossilized, too. The study of fossils, called paleontology, shows us that life began on Earth more than 3.5 billion years ago.

Only bones
Often the only remains of an animal are hard bones. This fossilized vertebra is from a plesiosaur, an ancient swimming reptile.

Packed tightly
Some fossils are densely packed because the animals were buried in large numbers. These ammonites are in limestone.

Plesiosaur tooth

Tough tooth
Teeth are often fossilized as they are hard.

Rare delicacy
Detailed fossils of dead plants are rare because plants rot quickly. However, the veins in this leaf have been preserved.

Pearly ammonite
Ammonites are now extinct. They were animals that had hard shells made of a chalky mineral called aragonite.

Opalized wood
One type of fossilization occurs when chemical changes make a mineral grow to replace the original animal or plant tissues. The tissues of this fossilized wood have been replaced by opal.

False fossil

This is not a fossil. The treelike growths, called dendrites, are deposits of a mineral called manganese within the rock.

Unnatural burial

This ancient Greek pot was found in the ground, but it is not a fossil. Fossil, which means "something dug up," once applied to buried pottery and minerals, but these are no longer considered fossils.

Area where fragments are missing

Ancient trail

This image shows the trail of an animal that moved across the seabed millions of years ago. Fossilized evidence of animal activities are called trace fossils.

Easy mistake

These images do not show a fossilized duck's head and a human leg! Their resemblance is pure chance. They are really lumps of rock called flint nodules found in chalk. The shapes of flint nodules can be very peculiar and they are often mistaken for fossils.

Flint "duck's head"

Flint "human leg"

Are minerals fossils?

No, minerals are not the remains of an animal or plant and are therefore not fossils.

"Squid-like creature"

Beringer's "Lying Stones"

"Bunch of grapes"

Fossil fakes

During the 1720s, when the nature of fossils was unclear, these "fossils" were carved and buried in the ground by people trying to fool a German scientist named Johann Beringer. He was taken in and published descriptions of his finds, but was later humiliated when the hoax was revealed.

Layer upon layer
The Grand Canyon is a natural slice through Earth's crust, which exposes layers of eroded sandstone and limestone. The oldest layer is at the bottom.

The making **of rocks**

The rocks beneath us have been forming for 4.6 billion years. Earth's crust is made up of elements, particularly oxygen, silicon, iron, and aluminum. These combine to form minerals, which in turn combine to make rocks. They can be igneous, metamorphic, or sedimentary.

Twisted trilobite
Metamorphic rocks may contain distorted fossils, such as this trilobite in slate.

Molten rocks
Igneous rocks are formed by the cooling of molten magma. Magma may erupt from volcanoes before it cools, but cooling often occurs underground.

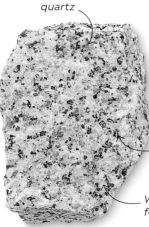

Glassy quartz

Black mica

White feldspar

Granite
Granite is an igneous rock formed at great depths.

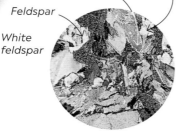

Feldspar *Mica* *Quartz*

Thin section of granite

Hot rocks
Heat and pressure create metamorphic rocks. Marble is metamorphosed limestone, while slate is metamorphosed shale.

Band rich in mica *Band rich in quartz*

Schist
Parallel bands of minerals feature in metamorphic rocks. Schist forms from shale or mud.

Band of quartz

Band of silicate minerals

Thin section of schist

Conglomerate
This sedimentary rock consists of pebbles bound by a natural mineral cement.

Pebble *Natural cement*

Sandstone

GEOLOGICAL TIME

A series of eras, periods, and epochs divide Earth's geological history.

Era	Period	Million years ago (MYA)
Cenozoic	Holocene (Epoch)	0.01
	Pleistocene (Epoch)	2.6
	Pliocene (Epoch)	5
	Miocene (Epoch)	23
	Oligocene (Epoch)	34
	Eocene (Epoch)	56
	Paleocene (Epoch)	66
Mesozoic	Cretaceous	145
	Jurassic	201
	Triassic	252
Paleozoic	Permian	299
	Carboniferous	359
	Devonian	419
	Silurian	444
	Ordovician	485
	Cambrian	539
	Precambrian (about nine times longer than all the other periods put together)	4,600 (formation of Earth)

Deposited rocks
Rocks are continually being eroded, creating grains carried by river, sea, or wind. They are deposited, together with the remains of animals and plants, as mud, sand, or coarser material. When this sediment is buried deeper, it becomes compacted and cemented to form sedimentary rock.

Quartz

Iron-rich cement

Thin section of sandstone

Sandstone
Sandstone is a sedimentary rock composed mainly of quartz sand.

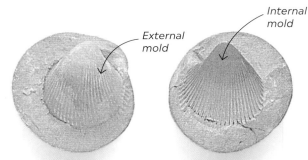

External mold

Internal mold

Fossil container
Many sedimentary rocks contain hard lumps called concretions or nodules, which sometimes contain fossils. In the fossil above, the shell has left an external mold of the outside of the shell and an internal mold of the insides.

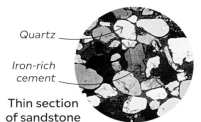

Fossil brachiopod

Fossiliferous rock
Limestone is a sedimentary rock composed of calcite and other carbonate minerals. The calcite is derived from the shells and skeletons of marine animals and plants. This Silurian limestone contains fossil brachiopods (see pp.24–25).

Turning to stone

The process of changing from a living organism to a fossil can take millions of years. As soon as animals and plants die, they begin to rot. Hard parts, such as the shells, bones, and teeth of animals, or the wood of plants, last longer than soft tissue, but they are often scattered by animals, wind, or water. For fossilization to take place, an animal or plant must be buried quickly by sediment. Only a tiny fraction will ever be fossilized, and even fewer will be found.

Land shapes
Over millions of years rocks are eroded, bringing ancient fossils to the surface.

2 Decaying mussel
When a mussel dies, its shell opens out into a "butterfly" position. The soft parts of the mussel inside the shell begin to rot, or are eaten by animals.

Living mussel

Byssal threads

1 Living mussels
Mussels live in the sea, attached to rocks by byssal threads. Dense masses form mussel beds. If a mussel becomes detached, it may die.

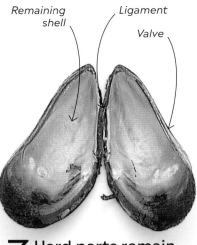

Remaining shell
Ligament
Valve

3 Hard parts remain

When the soft parts of the mussel have rotted away, the shell is all that remains.

FROM PRESERVATION TO DISCOVERY

These four drawings show how animals can be preserved and their remains discovered millions of years later. It is a slow process, and the climate and shape of the land will change as much as the animal and plant life.

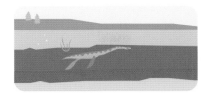

1. Dead animals sink to the seabed and the remains are buried by layers of sediment.

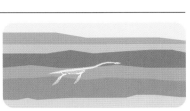

2. Lower layers of sediment turn to rock, and the animal remains become fossils.

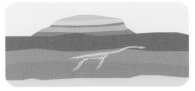

3. The rock is folded and eroded.

4. The fossils are exposed on the surface.

4 Toward fossilization

The shells of dead mussels are carried along and dropped by water currents, where they are mixed with pebbles and sand to form "mussel beaches." Some dead mussels have two valves held together by tough tissue called ligament, but in others, this has broken and the valves have separated. The sea can break shells into small pieces. These may become buried and eventually fossilized.

Separated shell

Tough ligament holding valves together

Fossil mussel shell

5 Fossilized mussels

Mussel shells can become buried in sediment and fossilized. Here, mineral cement binds sediment grains and shells together.

Blue fossils

The shells of living mussels are blue. Some color remains in these fossil mussels, which are 2 million years old.

Lost color

The color in shells is usually lost during fossilization. The brown in these fossils comes from the rock in which the shells were found.

Changing world

Our planet has been changing since it formed about 4.6 billion years ago. Earth's crust is divided into different moving plates. Most earthquakes and volcanoes occur along boundaries between these plates. Over time, small plate movements have caused continents to drift, to collide and form mountains, or to break into pieces. Sea levels and climates have changed constantly. The maps below show the land at four different stages in geological history. The fossils show examples of the life existing in each time span.

Continuous change

The earthquakes and volcanoes in Earth's recent history, such as the great earthquake of Lisbon, Portugal, in 1755, prove that changes are still taking place on Earth.

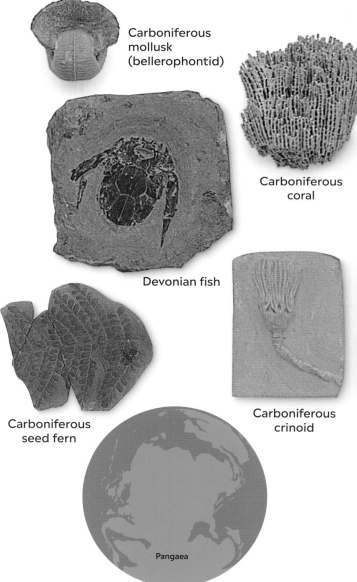

Carboniferous mollusk (bellerophontid)

Carboniferous coral

Devonian fish

Carboniferous crinoid

Carboniferous seed fern

Old fossils

The oldest fossils are bacteria-like cells 3.5 billion years old. This Australian *Tribrachidium* appeared in the late Precambrian.

Silurian graptolites

Silurian trilobites

Silurian gastropod

Silurian brachiopods

Gondwana

Pangaea

Early Paleozoic World (539–419 MYA)

Paleozoic means "ancient life." In the early Paleozoic Era (Cambrian, Ordovician, and Silurian periods), a large continent, known as Gondwana, was situated over the southern polar region. Most early Paleozoic life was in the ocean, which covered much of the planet.

Late Paleozoic World (419–252 MYA)

Life diversified in the late Paleozoic Era (Devonian, Carboniferous, and Permian periods). Reptiles, insects, and other animals colonized the land. Most land became joined in one supercontinent, called Pangaea. A mass extinction occurred at the end of the era.

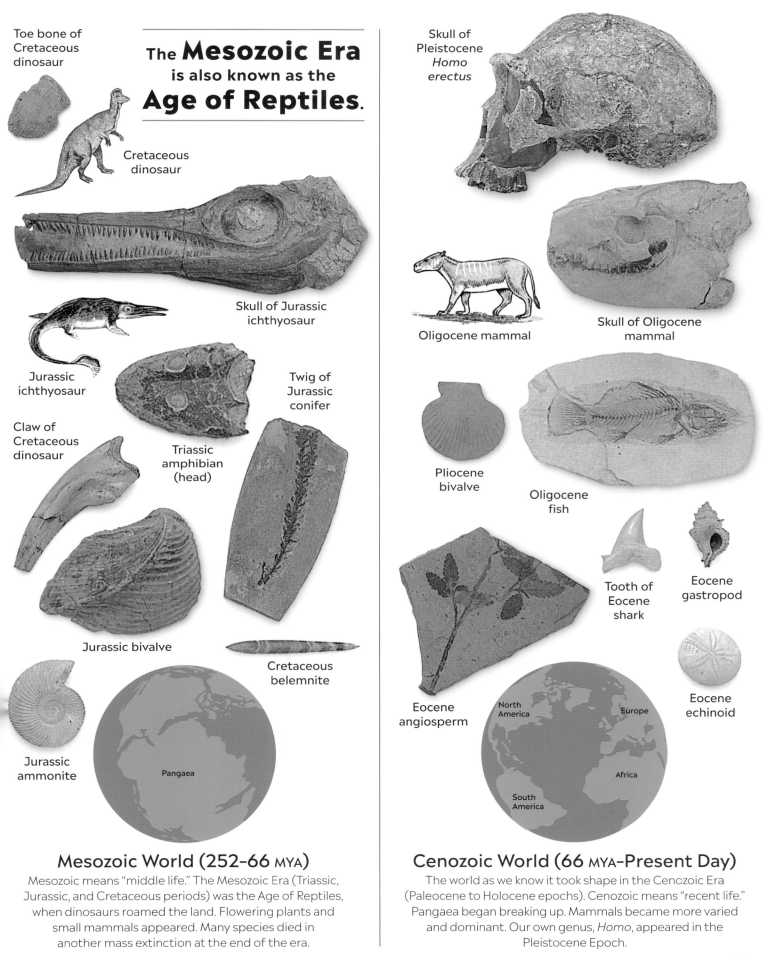

Toe bone of Cretaceous dinosaur

Cretaceous dinosaur

The **Mesozoic Era** is also known as the **Age of Reptiles**.

Skull of Jurassic ichthyosaur

Jurassic ichthyosaur

Twig of Jurassic conifer

Claw of Cretaceous dinosaur

Triassic amphibian (head)

Jurassic bivalve

Cretaceous belemnite

Jurassic ammonite

Pangaea

Skull of Pleistocene *Homo erectus*

Oligocene mammal

Skull of Oligocene mammal

Pliocene bivalve

Oligocene fish

Tooth of Eocene shark

Eocene gastropod

Eocene echinoid

Eocene angiosperm

North America

Europe

South America

Africa

Mesozoic World (252–66 mya)

Mesozoic means "middle life." The Mesozoic Era (Triassic, Jurassic, and Cretaceous periods) was the Age of Reptiles, when dinosaurs roamed the land. Flowering plants and small mammals appeared. Many species died in another mass extinction at the end of the era.

Cenozoic World (66 mya–Present Day)

The world as we know it took shape in the Cenozoic Era (Paleocene to Holocene epochs). Cenozoic means "recent life." Pangaea began breaking up. Mammals became more varied and dominant. Our own genus, *Homo*, appeared in the Pleistocene Epoch.

Early paleontology

The scientific study of fossils began about 300 years ago, although early Greek philosophers perhaps realized the true nature of fossils in the 5th century BCE. During the Middle Ages in Europe, many naturalists thought fossils were the products of a mysterious "plastic force" ("*vis plastica*"), which formed the fossils within Earth. Their true origin as the buried remains of ancient animals and plants was established by 17th-century naturalists. In today's world, our understanding of fossils continues to grow.

Georges Cuvier

French naturalist Georges Cuvier (1769–1832) realized that the parts of an animal's body were closely interrelated; for example, mammals with horns and hoofs were all herbivores and would have had herbivore teeth. This meant entire animals could be described from the evidence of isolated bones.

Noah's Ark

The Bible story of Noah tells how he took animals to his ark to escape the flood. Many naturalists thought this flood had taken and buried fossils. This explained why fossil seashells occurred on mountains.

Animals making their way to the ark

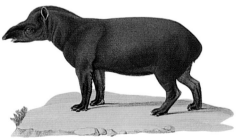

Restoration

Cuvier studied *Palaeotherium* bones from the Eocene rocks of Paris. The animal from which they came was restored as this tapir-like mammal.

Louis Agassiz

Swiss American biologist Louis Agassiz (1807–1873) showed that some young rocks, widely believed to be deposits formed by the Biblical Flood, had been deposited by glaciers during the Pleistocene Ice Age.

Fossil jaw of Palaeotherium

Grinding teeth of a herbivore

Steno

A court physician in Italy, Danish doctor Niels Stensen or Steno (1638–1686) was one of the first to realize the true nature of fossils. In 1667, he noticed that the teeth of a live shark were similar to "tongue stones" (below). Two years later, he would publish a book in which he stated that fossils were remains of ancient organisms.

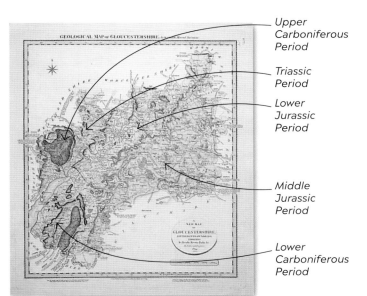

Upper Carboniferous Period

Triassic Period

Lower Jurassic Period

Middle Jurassic Period

Lower Carboniferous Period

Tongue stones

Fossil shark teeth from Cenozoic rocks around the Mediterranean, such as the ones to the right, were known to naturalists as "tongue stones."

First useful map

William Smith traveled extensively across Britain and produced the first British geological maps.

Gastropod

Bivalve hinge

Gastropod

Gastropod

Bivalve

1. *Inoceramus Cuvieri. Thoma Arnold. V. sp.448.* 4. *Ammonites.* 7. *Terebratula.*
2. *Inoceramus.* 5. *Cirrus depressus. Sowerby. M.B.* 8. *Terebratula subundata. M.C.t.83.f.7.*
3. *Cast of the inside of a Trochus.* 6. *Terebratula.* 9. *Sharks teeth.*

William Smith

English surveyor William Smith (1769–1839) collected fossils from different rock formations across England. Some of the fossils he collected can be seen here, along with plates from the books in which he illustrated his finds. He found that layers of rock were characterized by particular species of fossils and realized that rocks containing the same fossil species must be the same age.

Engraving of "Oak Tree Clay Fossils" by William Smith, 1816

Ammonite

Fossil folklore

Fossils are rich in folklore. For at least 10,000 years, fossils have been featured in the beliefs, legends, and customs of ordinary people around the world. Even today, many people believe that particular types of fossils have supernatural or medicinal powers. Some fossils were also valued for their rarity or natural beauty. The origin of fossils was mysterious to people for a long time and led to some strange ideas about them.

Carved snake's head

Whitby coat of arms

Ancient Whitby coin

Snakestone (ammonite)

Snakestones

Ammonites from Whitby in England were said to be the remains of coiled snakes turned to stone by 7th-century abbess, St. Hilda. Craftsmen carved heads on some ammonites. Three snakestones are shown in the Whitby coat of arms on this coin.

Devil's toenail

The Jurassic oyster *Gryphaea* had a thick curved shell, which is known as a Devil's toenail. This explanation was given despite the fact that the Devil is usually described as having hoofs, not toes!

Magic stones

Some people thought that fossil sea urchins were thunderstones fallen in a storm. One type was said to be a hardened ball of froth made by snakes at midsummer. The snakes tossed them in the air and if one was caught in a cloth, it had magical powers.

Thunderstones (fossil sea urchins)

Woodcut from 1497

👁 EYEWITNESS

Adrienne Mayor
US historian Adrienne Mayor has researched how myths in ancient cultures rose from fossil finds. For example, she found that ancient people based the shape of the mythical griffin on fossils of the dinosaur *Protoceratops*.

Old toad's tale

Toadstones are fossil teeth of the extinct fish *Lepidotes*. They get their strange name because people in medieval Europe wrongly believed they came from the head of a toad. Some even thought that placing a toad on red cloth would make it cough up the stones. They were thought to have healing properties.

Lucky spines

The spines of the sea urchin *Balanocidaris* (above), were considered lucky charms in ancient times. They are found in Mesozoic rocks of an area in the Middle East once known as Judea.

Toadstones (fossil fish teeth)

Famous myth

This French tapestry, called *The Lady and the Unicorn*, dates from 1500 CE. In medieval folklore, a unicorn horn was believed to be able to detect poison and make it harmless. Narwhal or fossilized mammoth tusks were often mistaken for unicorn horns.

Real unicorn

For many years, the tusk of a small whale called the narwhal was identified as the horn of the unicorn. However, the discovery in about 1600 of some fossil mammoth tusks (such as the one on the right) led to these being proclaimed as the true horns of unicorns, or *unicornum verum*!

Thunderbolts

The internal shells of extinct, squidlike animals called belemnites were said to have medicinal properties. They were believed to fall as darts from the heavens during storms.

Sponge beads

Bronze-Age people in Britain made necklaces by stringing together fossil sponges. Specimens of the Cretaceous sponge *Porosphaera* look like beads, and many have a hole in the middle.

Porosphaera

Take one shell

In China, the fossil shells of certain brachiopods are called *Shiy-yen* (stone swallows) and were used as medicine until recently. The prescription supplied with these Devonian brachiopods states they should be ground up, baked in a clay pot, and used as a cure for many illnesses.

京都 永仁堂

總魏北平五府并大街下

石燕 甘京

支居烟台北大街電話四

去湿止帯下

主赤白帯下

治腸風痔瘻

眼目諸

Stone swallow (fossil brachiopod)

Fossils of the future

The fossil record is a highly selective sample of ancient life. Many creatures did not have resistant hard parts and rotted away. Some lived where fossilization was unlikely to occur, such as in treetops. Only a small proportion of life became fossilized. This selectivity is illustrated by looking at a modern community to see which animals and plants may become fossils in the future.

Ray egg case

Cushion star

Brittlestar

Scallop

Mackerels

Scallop

Snail

Spiny starfish

Shrimp

Common starfish

Sea mouse

Snail egg case

Sponge

Bryozoan colony

Mackerel skeletons

Dogfish teeth | Crab shell

Scallop shells

Green sea urchin skeleton

Snail shell

Edible sea urchin skeleton

Common starfish skeleton

Cushion star skeleton

Spiny starfish skeleton

Brittlestar skeleton

Bryozoan skeleton

Temporary tenant

A good example of a creature that is unlikely to leave direct evidence of its existence is the hermit crab. Hermit crabs are unusual in having no shell of their own, instead using old snail shells as homes. Much of a hermit crab's body is soft and it twists in the spiral of the snail shell. The claws are hard but are rarely fossilized because they decay and disintegrate.

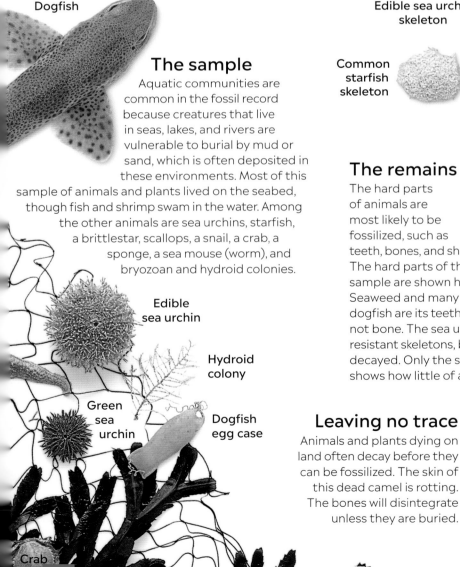

Dogfish

The sample

Aquatic communities are common in the fossil record because creatures that live in seas, lakes, and rivers are vulnerable to burial by mud or sand, which is often deposited in these environments. Most of this sample of animals and plants lived on the seabed, though fish and shrimp swam in the water. Among the other animals are sea urchins, starfish, a brittlestar, scallops, a snail, a crab, a sponge, a sea mouse (worm), and bryozoan and hydroid colonies.

Edible sea urchin

Hydroid colony

Green sea urchin

Dogfish egg case

Crab

The remains

The hard parts of animals are most likely to be fossilized, such as teeth, bones, and shells. The hard parts of the sample are shown here.

Seaweed and many creatures have disappeared. All that remains of the dogfish are its teeth. A dogfish has a skeleton of nonresistant cartilage, not bone. The sea urchins, starfish, brittlestar, crab, and bryozoans had resistant skeletons, but these fell apart as the tissues connecting them decayed. Only the snail and scallop shells have hardly changed. This shows how little of a modern community would survive to be fossilized.

Leaving no trace

Animals and plants dying on land often decay before they can be fossilized. The skin of this dead camel is rotting. The bones will disintegrate unless they are buried.

Remarkable remains

Occasionally, fossils of soft tissues, which usually decay during fossilization, are found. These include soft-bodied animals that are otherwise unrepresented in the fossil record. Fossilization of soft parts provides more information than bones, teeth, or shells.

Buried in ash

In the eruption of Mount Vesuvius, Italy, in 79 CE, some inhabitants of the nearby towns of Pompeii and Herculaneum were buried beneath avalanches of volcanic ash. The ash hardened around the bodies and the bodies decayed, leaving cavities. The victims' bodies have been revealed by filling excavated cavities with plaster to make casts. Around 1,100 bodies have been excavated at Pompeii so far.

Sticky end

A fly can be seen in this amber, the fossilized resin of an ancient plant. Amber often contains animals trapped in the sticky resin. Insects and frogs have been preserved for millions of years in this way.

Exceptional insect

This Jurassic dragonfly is from the Solnhofen Limestone located in Germany.

👁 EYEWITNESS

C. D. Walcott
US paleontologist Charles Doolittle Walcott (1850–1927) discovered the Burgess Shale deposit in British Columbia, Canada, in 1909. He visited this Cambrian rock many times, often with his family, and collected more than 65,000 fossils from it, many of which were of new and unusual species.

Amazing discovery

This unusual worm is from a deposit called the Burgess Shale, famous for its soft-bodied fossils. Other animals discovered in the Burgess Shale include trilobites and crustaceans. These animals were buried in mudflows on the Cambrian seabed 508 million years ago.

Soft preservation

Belemnoteuthis from the Jurassic Period is related to squid, cuttlefish, and the extinct belemnites. The skeleton of this specimen is hidden beneath the soft body, which has been preserved because of replacement by the mineral apatite soon after death and burial.

Hooked tentacles

Preserved soft body hides the internal skeleton

Grauballe Man

Human bodies in remarkable states of preservation have been excavated from European peat bogs. Acid prevented the total decay of soft parts. This man from the 4th century BCE was found near Grauballe village in Denmark with his skin and organs preserved.

Reconstruction of a moa

Stuck fast

Sticky tar oozing naturally to the surface at La Brea in Los Angeles, California, has accidentally trapped many animals for at least 10,000 years. Excavations in the older, solidified layers of tar have unearthed the bones of extinct mammals, such as mammoths. Here, a model of a mammoth is shown partly sunk in tar.

Skin

Bone

Fossil moa foot

Flightless moa

The moas of New Zealand were large, flightless birds related to the emu and ostrich. The biggest was 12 ft (3.6 m) tall. Now extinct, moas were alive when the Māori people first lived in New Zealand 700 years ago. Fossils of many species of moa have been found, some more than 15 million years old.

Claw

Corals

The colorful massed tentacles of coral individuals, or polyps, resemble flowers in an undersea garden. Most corals live in tropical waters and feed on plankton. Corals may be solitary (living alone) or colonial (many polyps joined together). Fossil corals are common because beneath the soft-bodied polyps are hard, chalky skeletons.

Red limestone

Pipe coral

The pipe-shaped corallites (skeletons formed by individual polyps) of this Carboniferous coral colony, *Siphonodendron*, grew separately. Spaces between them are now filled with red limestone.

Corallite (individual coral skeleton)

Coral fishing

Coral has long been collected for its beauty and is used in jewelry.

Horn coral

Aulophyllum is a solitary coral seen here in two parts. The pointed end was buried in seabed sediment, while the soft polyp sat on the other end.

Crammed colony

This colonial coral, *Lonsdaleia*, belongs to the Rugosa group. Rugose corals became extinct in the Permian Period. The corallites are many-sided and packed together.

Chain coral

This Silurian coral, *Halysites*, has corallites in branching ribbons. On the surface, it looks like a collection of chains.

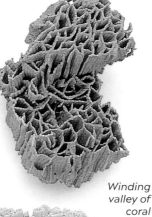

Brain coral

Together, the individuals of brain corals form winding valleys and the colonies resemble human brains. This Miocene example has been cut and polished.

Winding valley of coral

Pale sediment filling areas once occupied by soft tissues

Coral bush

Colonies of this coral, *Thamnopora*, are bush-shaped with corallites opening over the branches. This one in limestone has been cut horizontally and polished to show the colony shape.

Branch of corallites

Largest coral

This fossilized fragment of coral is the reef-building coral *Galaxea*. The world's largest-known living coral is a *Galaxea* colony from Okinawa in Japan, with a circumference of 52 ft (16 m).

Individual corallite

Replaced coral

Some fossil corals have skeletons made of the mineral aragonite. This dissolves easily, so the skeletons often disappear in fossilization. In this fossil colony of *Thecosmilia*, the skeleton has been replaced by silica.

Skeleton replaced by silica

Fossil *Fungia*

Fossil *Stephanophyllia*

Solitary corals

These fossils are the skeletons of solitary corals *Stephanophyllia* and *Fungia*, which lived on the seabed in the Pliocene and Pleistocene epochs, respectively. The skeletons of *Fungia* look like the undersides of mushrooms.

Modern corals

Most modern corals belong to a group called the scleractinians, which first appeared in the Triassic Period. Coral reefs are the most diverse marine environments of all.

Seabed dwellers

The most common fossils are of animals and plants that lived on the seabed. They were buried by sand and mud, and most had hard parts that could survive decay and be fossilized. Plants and many animals were buried because they did not move. Bryozoans and brachiopods are living examples. There are 350 known species of brachiopods living today, but 12,000 known fossil species.

Holes in the colony through which water and food particles are pumped

Community homes
The branching shape of this modern bryozoan, *Retihornera*, provides a home for worms, fish, and other marine life.

Close neighbors
Bryozoan colonies can be compared to apartments and other buildings containing several similar homes.

Individual skeleton

Larger than life
Part of a bryozoan colony is shown magnified here.

Curious colonies

Bryozoans are tiny animals that live in colonies in which each individual is attached to its neighbor. A colony may house thousands of individuals, each one less than 0.04 in (1 mm) long. They have tentacles to feed on tiny pieces of food. Most have skeletons made of calcite. Some colonies are flat sheets, while others grow upright.

Old lace
The lace bryozoan (*Chasmatopora*) in this Ordovician shale is among the oldest known bryozoans.

Archimedes's screw
This distinctive Carboniferous bryozoan is named after a spiral water pump invented by Greek scientist Archimedes because of its screw-shaped skeleton.

Each piece is a colony containing at least 200 individuals.

Free-living colonies of Cretaceous bryozoans

Red stone
The red of this Jurassic alga, *Neosolenopora*, has been preserved. The rock containing this fossil is known as beetroot stone.

Light and dark growth bands

Shells on stalks

Brachiopods have shells with two valves and can be mistaken for bivalve mollusks. One of the valves is larger than the other, whereas in bivalves the two valves are mirror images. The soft parts of bivalve mollusks are also different.

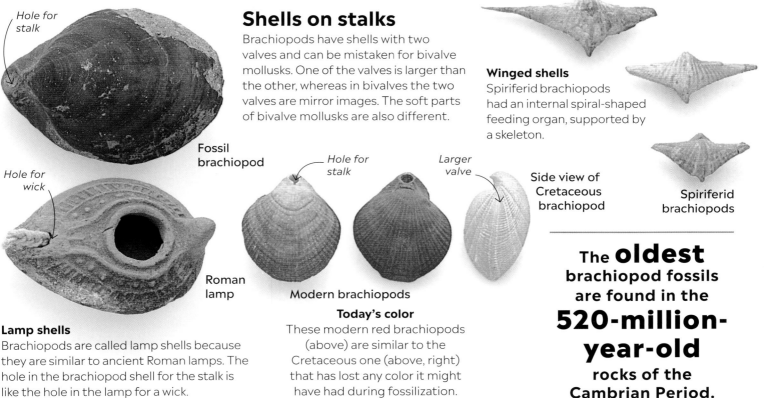

Hole for stalk

Fossil brachiopod

Hole for stalk

Larger valve

Side view of Cretaceous brachiopod

Winged shells
Spiriferid brachiopods had an internal spiral-shaped feeding organ, supported by a skeleton.

Spiriferid brachiopods

Roman lamp

Hole for wick

Lamp shells
Brachiopods are called lamp shells because they are similar to ancient Roman lamps. The hole in the brachiopod shell for the stalk is like the hole in the lamp for a wick.

Modern brachiopods

Today's color
These modern red brachiopods (above) are similar to the Cretaceous one (above, right) that has lost any color it might have had during fossilization.

The **oldest** brachiopod fossils are found in the **520-million-year-old** rocks of the Cambrian Period.

Sponges

Sponges are a primitive group of animals that pump water through their bodies. Sponge skeletons have small spicules, which can often be fossilized. Fossil sponges first occurred in the Cambrian Period.

Polished fossil of *Siphonia* sponge

Sponges without hard skeletons include the natural bath sponge

Fossil tulip sponge
(*Siphonia tulipa*)

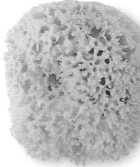

Modern branching sponge

Skeleton cup
Skeletons of sponges with fused spicules can be fossilized. Many are cup-shaped like this Cretaceous example (left).

Shell shapes

At the start of the Cambrian Period, about 539 million years ago, complex animals with hard shells and skeletons appeared in the sea. Among them were mollusks, a group still abundant today. Gastropods, or snails, and bivalves such as mussels, clams, and oysters are the most familiar mollusks, but others include chitons and cephalopods. The calcite or aragonite shells of mollusks are often found as fossils.

Ancient jewels
This mudstone contains rare fossil pearls.

Hinge tooth

Hinged together
Hinge teeth helped hold a bivalve's shells together. This was from an Eocene bivalve, *Venericor*.

Fall apart
These fossilized shells belong to the scallop *Chesapecten*, from the Pliocene Epoch. The ribs on the two shells interlock, but the shells often separate after death.

Geerat Vermeij
Dutch-born paleontologist Geerat Vermeij has lived in the US since the age of 10. Blinded at the age of 3, he uses the sense of touch to study modern and fossil shells, shedding new light on the evolution of mollusks.

Sensory tentacles   *Eye*   *Shell*   *Gape*

Good eyesight
Scallops have many eyes, each with well-developed lenses. They sit in soft tissue by the shell edge. Scallop shells are hinged together. To feed, they use their gills to cause a current of water laden with food particles to pass through the shell gape.

Disappearing color
Some living gastropods, especially those in the tropics, are brightly colored. Their color is due to pigment, a chemical substance within the shell. These colorful snails are from Cuba. Pigments are usually destroyed during fossilization.

Twisting coils
Gastropod shells of all ages come in different shapes and sizes. They are all open at one end, increasing in diameter as they twist into a spiral coil. The spiral shape can be left-handed, right-handed, loosely coiled, or tightly coiled. *Turritella* (right) has a shell that is drawn out into a high spire.

Fossil snail shell

Irregularly coiled shell

"Worm shells"
Vermetids are unusual gastropods that attach themselves to a hard surface, often in clusters like these fossils. Their shells resemble worm tubes.

Turritella *shell is made of calcium carbonate*

No connection
Chitons are a small group of marine mollusks with shells made up of eight individual plates. Fossil chitons are rare and their plates are disconnected. Today chitons can be found in rock pools, sticking to the rocks from which they scrape algae for food.

Fossil chiton

Fine growth lines

Fossil *Turritella*

Extra long
The *Fusinus* shell has a siphonal canal used in respiration.

Siphonal canal

Left-handed coil

Fossil *Neptunea despecta*

Right-handed coil

Modern chiton

Fossil *Neptunea angulata*

Right or left?
Most gastropods have shells with a right-handed spiral coil, such as *Neptunea despecta*.

Loose coils
Tubina is a mollusk belonging to an extinct group, the bellerophontids. It has a loosely coiled shell and dates back to the Devonian Period.

27

Mighty mollusks

Pyritized ammonite shell

The octopus, squid, and cuttlefish are modern representatives of a group of sea-dwelling mollusks called cephalopods, which have left a rich fossil record. They are the most highly developed mollusks, with suckered arms, advanced eyes, and the ability to learn. They are active predators, moving quickly through the water using jet propulsion. Following their first appearance in the Cambrian Period, many species came and went, making them useful fossils for dating rocks.

Important evidence

The living *Nautilus* is the closest relative of the ammonites and provides information about this extinct group. *Nautilus* is a nocturnal animal, active at night, and lives in the Pacific and Indian oceans at depths of up to 2,300 ft (700 m). It eats fish and crustaceans.

Ammonite art

Ammonites are used in decoration. This column is from a house in Brighton, England. The architect was named Amon!

Various sizes

Some Mesozoic ammonites reached gigantic sizes. This large specimen, 12 in (30 cm) wide, is small compared to giants that could be 5 ft 9 in (1.75 m) in diameter.

Final chamber

Septa dividing shell into chambers

Complex suture line

Ammonites

Simple suture line

Fossil nautiloids

Rooms for expansion

Fossil ammonites and nautiloids have coiled shells divided into chambers by septa. Only the last chamber was occupied by the animal. As it grew, the animal moved forward and formed new septa. Older chambers filled with liquid and gas to let the animal move up and down in the sea. Suture lines where the septa meet the shell are simple in nautiloids but complex (wavy) in ammonites.

Male
ammonite

A real
pagoda
in China

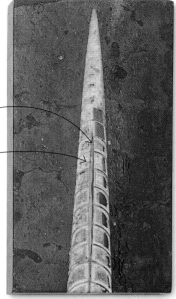

*Siphuncle
linking the
chambers*

Chamber

Unlikely pair

Male and female
ammonites of the
same species often
had different shells.
Female shells were
larger, and the opening
was a different shape.

Female
ammonite

Pagoda stone

A group of cephalopods called orthoceratoids had straight
or slightly curved external shells, which are common fossils
in Paleozoic rocks. This cut specimen shows the chambers
and the siphuncle. Fossils such as this one have been called
pagoda stones and were thought in Chinese folklore to be
caused by the shadows cast on the rock by real pagodas
(sacred Buddhist buildings having multiple stories).

Fools' gold

In these ammonites
from Jurassic rocks in
Germany, the shell has
been replaced by the mineral iron pyrite,
known as "fools' gold." Ammonites
had aragonite shells, which often
dissolved during fossilization.

*Coils on
different
planes*

*Coils going
in different
directions*

*Partly
uncoiled
shell*

Modern squid

Squid have horny, internal
shells shaped like a pen.
The longest squid
on record was
62 ft (19 m)!

Fossil
belemnite

*Internal
guard*

Inside guard

This fossil (above) is
the remains of an extinct
cephalopod called a belemnite.
Common in Jurassic and
Cretaceous rocks, belemnites
had squid-shaped bodies. Only
the bullet-shaped internal guard, an
internal shell, is normally preserved.

Reconstruction
of a belemnite

Irregular coils

The shells of most ammonites
are coiled tightly in one plane with
one whorl touching the next. However,
some look like snail shells, while others
are partly uncoiled. A few unusual
species feature coils going in
different directions.

Animals in armor

Insects, spiders, crabs, scorpions, and lobsters belong to a large group of animals called arthropods, meaning "jointed foot." They have jointed legs, a segmented body, and an exoskeleton, or outer armor. Some arthropods, such as the extinct trilobites, have the mineral calcite in their exoskeletons, which makes them resist decay. These exoskeletons are often found fossilized.

Prize piece
Trilobites are prized fossils. This Silurian *Calymene* has been made into a brooch. It was found in Dudley, England, and nicknamed the Dudley bug.

Modern millipede

Fossil millipede

Early settlers
Like all arthropods, millipedes have bodies divided into pieces, or segments. They were one of the first animals on land.

Trilobite *Concoryphe*

To see or not to see?
Around 10,200 species of trilobites once lived in the sea. Some swam and floated, while others crawled on the seabed. Most species had two eyes and good vision. Lenses can be preserved in fossil trilobites because they are made of calcite. Some species in the deep sea had no eyes.

Echinocaris, a Devonian, shrimplike arthropod

Trilobite *Dalmanites*

Small is beautiful
Most trilobites were 1–4 in (3–10 cm) long. These ones are *Elrathia*.

Roll up!
Some trilobites could roll up like woodlice, probably for protection against predators.

Tri-lobed
The name trilobite comes from the exoskeletons divided into three parts or lobes, with the axial lobe running down the center. Whole fossil trilobites can be found in rocks from the Cambrian to the Permian Period, about 545 to 248 million years old. *Paradoxides* from the Cambrian Period grew to 1 ft 7 in (50 cm) long.

Axial lobe

👁 EYEWITNESS

Rachel Wood
British paleontologist Rachel Wood studies the evolution of the first animals on Earth. She looks at fossils of the earliest animals with hard skeletons, such as sponges, as well as the oldest reefs in the ocean.

Lobster concretion

Lobsters belong to a group of arthropods called crustaceans. Though they have hard shells, crustaceans are rarely fossilized because their shells break down. This Eocene lobster, *Homarus*, has been preserved in a concretion.

Lobster's body

Lobster's claw

Folded claws

China crab

This Cenozoic fossil crab from China looks similar to its modern relative except it does not have the red coloration. The claws are folded in and parts of the legs have broken off.

Modern barnacle

Modern crab

Fossil sea scorpion

Sea scorpion

Terror of the sea

Eurypterids, better known as sea scorpions, were ferocious hunters in the Paleozoic Era. They are related to today's scorpions and some were more than 3 ft in size.

Armor-plated

Barnacles are a type of crustacean protected in a "shell" of hard plates. Barnacles wave their legs in the water to create a current that wafts food into their mouths. The plated shells of barnacles are often found as fossils, especially in Cenozoic rocks. This cluster of fossilized barnacles from New Zealand is 2 million years old.

Arms and spines

Echinoderms are a distinctive group of sea creatures, including sea urchins (echinoids), sea lilies (crinoids), starfish (asteroids), and brittlestars (ophiuroids). Most echinoderms have fivefold radial symmetry, meaning their bodies can be divided into five similar segments. As echinoderms have skeletons made of resistant calcite, they are often found fossilized.

Modern brittlestar

Delicate arms

Arm in arm
This Jurassic specimen shows a group of five fossil brittlestars with overlapping arms. Brittlestars look like starfish, but their arms break off easily—hence, their name. They use their arms to move across the seabed and to feed.

Starfish can sometimes grow an entire new body from a single severed arm.

Symmetrical arm

Mouth

Suckers

Underside of modern starfish

Arm robbery
This fossil starfish from the Jurassic, seen from underneath, is similar to modern species, but has lost an arm. Its mouth is in the center. The rock contains tiny ammonites and shell fragments.

Position of missing arm

Mouth

Ammonite

Modern *Protoreaster*

Star hunter
Many starfish are efficient hunters, often feeding on bivalves, which they open using arm suckers. Others, like this Australian *Protoreaster*, extract food from sediments such as sand.

Fossil test of a heart urchin—an "irregular" echinoid

Armed with clubs

This specimen of the Cretaceous sea urchin *Tylocidaris* has been partly extracted from a chalk block. Many club-shaped spines have been preserved.

Interlocking plates

Tests of modern, regular sea urchins

Needle-like spines

Club-shaped spine

Sea tests

Sea urchins have skeletons called tests made of interlocking plates. Some plates have spines, which vary in shape from needlelike to club-shaped. Many sea urchins have five teeth for munching algae and other food. Spines and jaws are usually missing in fossils. Heart urchins are "irregular" echinoids, with a distinct front and end—unlike regular echinoids. They live in burrows in sand or mud and extract food from the sediment.

Modern sea urchin

Fossil crinoid

Arms

Arms

Segmented stem

Fossil *Pentacrinites*

Modern sea lily

Flat fossil

Sand dollars are unusual echinoids as they have flattened tests, often with large holes. They live partly buried in the sand and get food from sediment. Sand dollars first appeared in the Paleocene Epoch and are still living in the shallow waters of warm seas.

Sea flowers

There is a rich fossil record of crinoids with stems. These animals were attached to hard surfaces by a long stem. Individuals of *Pentacrinites* hung upside down from driftwood. Stems were made of disc-shaped segments, and these are often found fossilized. Most crinoids today do not have stems. Known as featherstars, they crawl and swim using their arms. Stemmed species live in deep water. They look like flowering plants and are called sea lilies.

Segmented stem

Fish

Fish are the most primitive vertebrates (animals with backbones). They have gills to breathe and fins to swim. There are 30,000 species. Fish appeared about 500 million years ago. Most were small, jawless, and covered in armor. In the Devonian Period, called the Age of Fishes, they became plentiful. Skeletons of fossil fishes are found in specific areas, but it is more common to discover teeth.

Jaws
One of the first known fish with jaws was a group of armored fish called placoderms.

Shark spine
Sharks and rays have soft cartilage skeletons, which are not normally fossilized. They have teeth and spines that are resistant (don't decay quickly), with fossils dating to the Devonian Period

Ear stones
Otoliths are balance organs from the ears of fish. They are made of chalky material and form unusual fossils. These examples are from Eocene fishes.

Dorsal fin

Otodus megalodon chasing a young humpback whale

Shark teeth
Most sharks are fierce predators with sharp teeth. The largest recorded modern shark was a great white measuring 20 ft 9 6 m). However, its extinct relative, *Otodus megalodon* (right), had teeth that were 7 in (18 cm) long, suggesting a body length of 49 ft (15 m).

The massive jaws of a megalodon were lined with
276 teeth!

Tooth of *Otodus megalodon*

Jawless fish
Cephalaspids were primitive freshwater fish. They were jawless and fed by sucking sediment.

Ridges for crushing food

Ptychodus tooth

Shell crushers
Fossil teeth are all that have survived of a cartilaginous fish, *Ptychodus*, which was like a modern ray. Its ridged teeth crushed up mollusk shells.

Sparnodus part

Sparnodus counterpart

Two parts

This slab of Eocene limestone has split through a fossil specimen of *Sparnodus*. The two bits are the part and the counterpart. *Sparnodus* belongs to a group of bony fish alive today called porgies or sea breams.

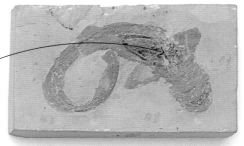

Swallowed fish head

Fish eats fish

Fossils rarely provide evidence of an animal's diet. However, this Cretaceous dogfish contains a teleost head that it swallowed. The dogfish had tiny teeth, so it probably scavenged the head from a fish that was already dead.

Otodus megalodon *had a short nose (rostrum).*

Acid exposure

The Devonian lungfish *Chirodipterus* had thick, bony scales. This Australian specimen was preserved in a chalky concretion and has been exposed by acid treatment, which dissolved the concretion but not the fish.

Thick scales

Armored head

Thick-scaled fish

Lepidotes was a Mesozoic bony fish. It was found all over the world and could grow to almost 6 ft 6 in (2 m). The body was covered in thick scales.

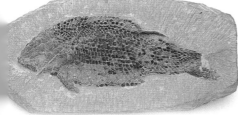

Bony fish

About 200 million years ago, this primitive teleost, a type of bony fish, lived in the ocean. Teleosts appeared in the Triassic, and today they are the most common type of fish. They include carp, salmon, cod, and mackerel.

Plant pioneers

The invasion of the land by plants about 430 million years ago was a key event in the history of life. It paved the way for colonization of land by animals and was the starting point for the plants we see today. Plants on land had to support themselves against gravity, be resistant to drying, and move water from the roots to the higher parts of the plants, where energy-producing photosynthesis occurred. These adaptations were first seen in primitive land plants of the Paleozoic Era.

Johann Scheuchzer

Swiss naturalist Johann Scheuchzer (1672–1733) studied fossil plants and fish from the Miocene rocks in Switzerland.

Impression in sandstone of the bark of *Lepidodendron*

Jet jewels

Jet is a fossil wood dense enough to carve and polish for jewelry. Jet formed when wood from monkey puzzle trees was washed into the sea.

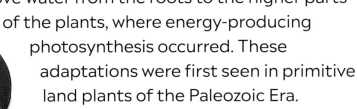

Cross section of the fossil cone *Lepidostrobus*

Carboniferous clubmoss *Archaeosigillaria*

Fossil *Baragwanathia*

Lepidodendron

Club mosses

Belonging to a plant group called lycopods, club mosses reproduce using spores held in cones. Lycopods were common in the Paleozoic Era. *Baragwanathia* from the Devonian, found in Australia, is the oldest example. Paleozoic lycopods grew as trees, with *Lepidodendron* stretching 130 ft (40 m).

Spores are produced at the base of leaves.

Modern club moss *Lycopodium*

👁 EYEWITNESS

Birbal Sahni

Indian paleobotanist Birbal Sahni (1891–1949) studied plant fossils in the Indian subcontinent. He found fossils of ferns such as *Glossopteris* that had been fossilized when the subcontinent was part of Gondwana (see p.12) during the Paleozoic Era.

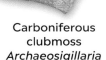

Starting seeds

The oldest ferns are of Devonian age. They are common fossils in Mesozoic rocks and about 10,000 species are alive today. They have spore cases on the underside of their leaves. Tree ferns such as *Psaronius* grew alongside club moss trees in the Coal Measure forests (see p.40). The leaves of the now-extinct seed ferns resemble true fern leaves, but they were, in fact, relatives of more advanced, seed-bearing plants.

Modern fern

Archaeopteris, an extinct tree that grew to 98 ft (30 m) tall

Compressed fern
Carbonized leaves of Jurassic fern *Coniopteris* have been preserved as compressions.

Familiar fern
Iodites from the Jurassic is a typical fern—the fronds are similar to those of modern species.

Plants in a Paleozoic forest

Polished fern
This piece of fossil wood is from the tree fern *Psaronius*, which reached 26 ft (8 m).

Fossil cones
This fossil monkey puzzle cone has been sectioned to show the internal structure.

Seed spread
The presence of fossils of this seed fern, *Glossopteris*, in India, Africa, South America, Australia, and Antarctica, prove these areas were once linked as Gondwana.

This image shows the only modern horsetail genus, *Equisetum*, which grows to 5 ft (1.5 m) tall.

Monkey puzzle
The monkey puzzle is a primitive conifer that appeared in the Triassic. Today it grows in the Andes mountains in South America.

Horsetails
Horsetails date back to the Devonian, reaching 60 ft (18 m). This is a Jurassic *Equisetites* stem.

Leaf-bearing part of stem

Modern monkey puzzle branch

Underground part of stem / *Equisetites*

Continued on next page **37**

Continued from previous page

Protected seeds

Most modern seed-producing plants have their seeds protected in a fruit (flowering plants or angiosperms) or a cone (gymnosperms, including conifers). Angiosperms are the most successful modern plants, having 300,000 species compared with 50,000 species of other plants. Angiosperms include grasses, oaks, tulips, potatoes, and cacti. They appear late in the fossil record. The earliest examples come from the Cretaceous Period.

Before flowers

When angiosperms first appeared, cycads were common plants. These palmlike gymnosperms produced seeds in separate conelike structures. Modern cycads still look like palms, and nine types live in tropical forests.

Annual rings preserved in stone

Palmlike leaf

Fossil cycad

Petrified conifer wood

Cycad companion

Other gymnosperms were also living at this time, and some Cretaceous conifer wood has been petrified (turned to stone). This has preserved details of the original wood.

Fossil palm

There are two main types of angiosperms—monocotyledons and dicotyledons. Generally, monocotyledons have leaves with parallel veins, while dicotyledons have net-veined leaves. Palms, like this *Sabal* from the Eocene, and grasses are monocotyledons. All other angiosperms shown are dicotyledons.

Leaf of a modern palm

Sabal leaf

Giant conifer

Giant redwoods are conifers found in North America. Conifers are gymnosperms and produce seeds inside cones. Fossils include rooted stumps, cones, and seeds.

Fossil poplar leaf

Juglans seeds

Tectocarya seeds

Palliopora seeds

Mastixia seeds

Modern poplar leaf

Small change

Fossil poplar leaves are almost identical to poplars today. This one is about 25 million years old. Modern poplar trees can grow to 130 ft (40 m) tall.

Ancient seeds

Angiosperm seeds are often enclosed in a fleshy fruit that animals eat before the seeds are dispersed. Various types of fossil fruits and seeds are common from the Late Cretaceous Period onward.

Split in two

Angiosperm leaves are well-preserved in some fine-grained sedimentary rocks. This Miocene example of a myrtle leaf has been fractured into two parts.

Fossil Miocene leaves

Fossil maple leaf showing midrib and veins

Leaf impressions

These Miocene leaves are preserved as impressions in limestone. The three-lobed leaf with midrib and delicate veins is a maple.

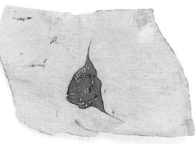

Leaves of a modern maple

Bud

In bud

Buds are rarely preserved in fossil plants, but one is attached to this Miocene maple tree.

Modern *Nipa* fruit

Flat chestnut

This is the flattened seed of a water chestnut from the Miocene Epoch.

Coast guards

A fruit of a modern *Nipa* tree is compared here with a smaller fossil *Nipa* fruit from the Eocene. *Nipa* is a stemless palm that grows along tropical coastlines.

Fossil *Nipa* fruit

Preserved petals

Fossils of flowers are seldom found, so these petals of *Porana* from the Miocene Epoch are exceptional. A flower today with similar petals is the primrose.

Fossil flower

Modern primrose

Fossil fuels

Oil and coal are called fossil fuels because they originate from ancient organisms, mainly plants. When burned, they release energy in the form of heat and light. However, the burning of fossil fuels releases carbon dioxide into the atmosphere, which causes global warming. This leads to extreme weather conditions and rising sea levels. We can reduce global warming by using renewable forms of energy such as solar and wind power.

1 Peat
These living plants will die and add their remains to the peat. Dried peat can be used as fuel in domestic fireplaces or in multifuel stoves.

From plant to coal

Coal forms after millions of years by the decay and burial of plants that grow in freshwater swamps. Special conditions are needed to form coal. At first, oxygen must not be present so that bacterial decay of the plants leads to the formation of peat. This is buried under more sediment and rotting plants. It undergoes chemical changes transforming into lignite, then bituminous coal, and finally, if temperatures and pressures are high enough, anthracite coal.

2 Lignite
The first stage of coal formation may still contain water. It crumbles easily and may crack as it dries in the air.

Coal plant
This impression of bark is of a plant from the Carboniferous Coal Measure forests. About two-thirds of the world's coal supply came from these plants.

3 Bituminous coal
Black bituminous coal is the most common coal used in homes. This impression of a Carboniferous lycopod tree shows the plant origin of the coal.

Ink

Shoe polish

Coal content
Most coal is burned to heat water into steam, which drives power station generators to produce electricity. In many parts of the world it is also burned to produce heat in domestic fireplaces. Many everyday products are also made from coal, such as ink and shoe polish.

4 Anthracite
Anthracite is a hard, intensely black and shiny coal. It is the best-quality coal.

From plankton to oil

Oil and natural gas are together known as petroleum, from the Latin words *petra* (rock) and *oleum* (oil). They were formed mainly by the decomposition of tiny planktonic plants that lived near the sea surface. When they died, their remains sank to the seabed and were buried in mud. Over millions of years, this mud turned to rock and the organic remains formed specks of carbon-rich kerogen, an early stage of oil, and then oil. Oil is often found far from where it originated. It moves upward through porous rocks that have tiny spaces into which it can seep.

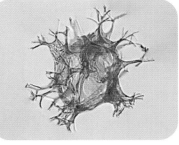

Oil plant
This fossil of a microscopic Eocene plant that lived in the sea has been greatly enlarged. Fossilized remains provide clues about rocks, which help geologists searching for oil.

Oil-bearing
This porous core contains oil. Oil is held as tiny droplets in rock pores—similar to the way water is held in a sponge.

No oil
This core of rock, cut during drilling for geologists to examine, does not contain any oil.

Heavy crude oil   Light crude oil

Crude oils
The presence of natural gas helps force oil to the surface, but sometimes pressure is too low and the oil must be pumped up. Crude oils (oils in their natural state) vary widely. The heaviest oils are black and thick. The lightest oils are pale and thin. All crude oils must be refined.

Refined oil
Oils are treated in a refinery. Refining is a complex process.

Polyester scarf

Sunglasses

Wax crayons

Made from oil
Once in the refinery, oil is separated into liquids, gases, and solids. These make a range of products in addition to petrol, diesel, and lubricating oil. Wax crayons, sunglasses, and polyester are all by-products of oil.

Oil rigs
Sometimes large reserves of oil are found deep beneath the seabed. To extract the oil, gigantic rigs are built out at sea where they drill down into the rocks of the seafloor. Many have legs that stretch hundreds of feet from the surface to the seafloor. Rigs have to be very strong in order to withstand high winds and huge waves.

Out of the water

Colonization of the land by vertebrates, 375 million years ago, was possible through the evolution of lungs for breathing air, and limbs for walking. Air-breathing was inherited by the first land vertebrates—amphibians—from their fish ancestors. Fish with lungs for breathing—lungfish—still exist today. Limbs for walking developed from muscular fins, like those of the living coelacanth (see pp.60–61).

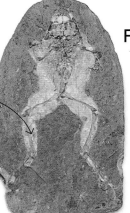

Fossil frog

This fossil frog is a female *Discoglossus* from Germany in the Miocene Epoch. Frogs appeared in the Triassic Period but are seldom found fossilized because their delicate bones decay.

Long hind legs

A 40-million-year-old **frog fossil** was discovered in **Antarctica**, suggesting that the area was once warm and **swamplike**.

Modern natterjack toad

Surviving amphibian

Early inhabitants of the land were very different from the amphibians that have survived today, such as frogs, toads, newts, and salamanders.

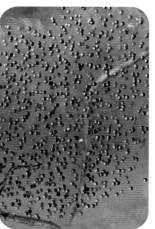

Going through stages

Like most amphibians, frogs lay their eggs in water. These hatch into tadpoles. They live in water as they develop into miniature frogs. Lungs and skin replace gills for breathing, fore- and hind legs grow, and the tail disappears.

Fish out of water

The mudskipper may be similar to the first amphibians in lifestyle. It lives in tropical mangrove swamps and can emerge from the water despite having no lungs, hauling itself around by its front fins.

Stunning skull

This well-preserved skull of an amphibian comes from Russia in the Triassic Period. *Benthosuchus* lived in fresh water, ate fish, and resembled a small crocodile.

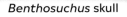

Benthosuchus skull

Modern group

Salamander

Salamanders belong to a modern group of amphibians called lissamphibians, which also includes newts and frogs.

Water world

The axolotl is an unusual salamander from Central America. It normally remains in a "larval" stage throughout its life, using its feathery external gills to breathe underwater and doesn't need to come onto land.

Skilled hunter

Eryops probably had a lifestyle similar to modern crocodiles. It was an aggressive meat-eater, which hunted for prey in water and on land.

Eryops skeleton

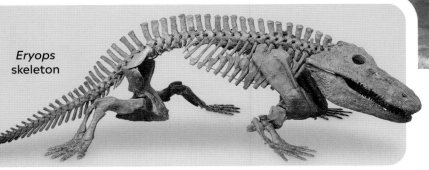

Sturdy skeleton

This skeleton belonged to *Eryops*, an amphibian of the Permian Period. Remains have been found in parts of the US. *Eryops* was a heavily built animal with strong bones and sharp teeth. It grew to 8 ft 2 in (2.5 m) long. The short, stout legs imply it probably lived mostly on land.

Early amphibian

Fossils of *Ichthyostega,* an early amphibian, are found in Devonian rocks in Greenland. It was able to walk on land, had lungs for breathing air, but still had a tail fin like a fish.

Onto the land

Three main types of reptiles live today: lizards and snakes, tortoises and turtles, and crocodiles. A fourth is represented only by the tuatara. The first reptile fossils date from the Carboniferous Period, about 310 million years ago. Early reptiles had two features, still seen in modern species, that meant they could live away from water. They developed a special egg, known as an amniote egg, and a scaly skin to prevent their bodies from drying out.

Bodyguard

Trionyx is a turtle from the Eocene. Only the protective carapace, or shell, is preserved here. The first turtles appeared in the Triassic Period and lacked the ability of modern species to withdraw their head, limbs, and tail completely.

Ready for land

Turtle eggs contain liquid and have leathery shells for protection. Before birth, an embryo can develop into a juvenile that can breathe and live on land.

Legless vertebrate

The earliest fossil snakes come from the middle Jurassic. Snakes have a poor fossil record, but vertebrae are occasionally found. These vertebrae of *Palaeophis* (below), from the Paleocene Epoch and found in Mali, were found separately, but have been assembled to give an idea of a snake's backbone. Snakes probably evolved from a lizardlike ancestor, with their limbs getting smaller and smaller and eventually disappearing.

Modern ladder snake

Laying eggs

Oceanic turtles move onto land to lay their eggs, which they bury in sand before returning to the sea. The largest living turtle is the leatherback (below), which reaches 8 ft (2.5 m) in length. But the Cretaceous turtle *Archelon* grew to more than 13 ft (4 m) in length!

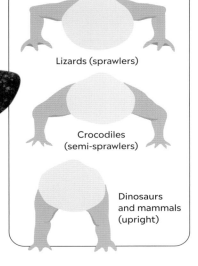
Archelon's shell
was the size of a
small car!

Long body

Scaly skin prevents drying out

Flattened skull

Powerful jaws

Crocodile head

This head belonged to an Oligocene crocodile, *Diplocynodon*. The largest fossil crocodile, *Deinosuchus*, from the Cretaceous Period and found in Texas, is estimated to have been 40–50 ft (12–15 m) long!

Diplocynodon skull

Baby predator

Crocodiles have changed little since the Jurassic—they all have long bodies, short legs, a flattened skull, and sharp teeth. Crocodiles are predators that swim slowly toward their prey before making a rapid grab using their powerful jaws.

Long lizard

Lizards live in dry, upland areas where burial is unlikely so fossil examples are rare. The earliest finds are from the Triassic Period, and they were probably present in vast numbers with their larger relatives, the dinosaurs. This fossil lizard, *Adriosaurus*, had a long body and is almost snakelike.

Sea reptiles

During Mesozoic times, when dinosaurs roamed the land, the seas were inhabited by giant reptiles. The most numerous were the ichthyosaurs (sea-dragons) and plesiosaurs, but a third group, the mosasaurs, became common near the end of the Mesozoic Era. They lived like modern marine mammals, such as small whales, dolphins, and seals. Some ate fish, while others ate belemnites and other mollusks. They all breathed air and so surfaced regularly.

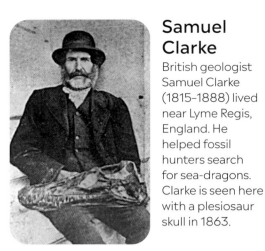

Samuel Clarke
British geologist Samuel Clarke (1815–1888) lived near Lyme Regis, England. He helped fossil hunters search for sea-dragons. Clarke is seen here with a plesiosaur skull in 1863.

Modern dolphins

Dorsal fin for stabilization

A good likeness
The shape of modern dolphins and ichthyosaurs suggests they shared a similar lifestyle.

Kink in backbone

Powerful tail for swimming

A mosasaur

Backbone

Giant lizard jaw
Three teeth are visible in this mosasaur jaw fragment from the Cretaceous Period. Mosasaurs were related to today's monitor lizards. They grew to 56 ft (17 m) and were slow-moving predators.

Pointed tooth

Excavation of a mosasaur jaw from a chalk mine at Maastricht in the Netherlands, in the 18th century

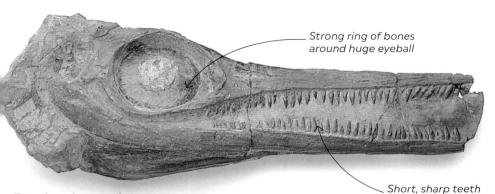
Strong ring of bones around huge eyeball

Short, sharp teeth

Packed teeth
The long jaws of most ichthyosaurs were full of sharp teeth. Nostrils were positioned far back on the top of the skull, as in modern dolphins and whales, making it easier to breathe when they surfaced for air. Large eyes helped in seeing clearly through the water.

Battle of the sea reptiles
This picture shows a fictitious fight between an ichthyosaur (left) and a plesiosaur (right).

Streamlined predator
The streamlined shape of an ichthyosaur is seen in this Jurassic specimen (left), where soft tissue has been preserved with the skeleton. The neck vertebrae of ichthyosaurs were close together so the head ran smoothly into the body. This is typical of fast-swimming predators and is seen in dolphins today. Ichthyosaurs swam by moving their tails. Their backbones had a kink and then continued into the lower part of the tail fin. The dorsal fin and paddles were used for steering and stability.

Neck vertebrae close together

Eye socket

Long jaws

Packed teeth

Paddle for steering

Main age
First appearing in the Triassic, ichthyosaurs were most common in the Jurassic.

Paddle power
The limbs of plesiosaurs formed large paddles. A plesiosaur, like a turtle, probably flapped these up and down for swimming.

Different plesiosaur species had different size flippers.

👁 EYEWITNESS

Mary Anning
British paleontologist Mary Anning (1799–1847) began collecting fossils near the cliffs of Lyme Regis from a very young age. Her many discoveries include a complete ichthyosaur skeleton and the world's first plesiosaur fossil.

Fossil giants

Dinosaurs provide the most impressive fossils of all. There were many species, and their reign spanned 150 million years from the Triassic to the Cretaceous. Dinosaurs were reptiles. Some ate meat, while others ate plants. Some had armored plates, others had feathers, and some had spiked or clubbed tails. The extinction of the dinosaurs at the end of the Cretaceous Period has prompted many extinction theories, the most popular being an asteroid impact.

Food-grinder

The Jurassic sauropod *Apatosaurus* weighed 33 tons. Like all sauropods, it was a plant-eater, using its long neck to reach treetops. It swallowed stones to help grind up food in the stomach, like crocodiles do today.

Apatosaurus had strong neck bones.

Plant-eater

One of the last-surviving dinosaurs was *Edmontosaurus*. It was a hadrosaur, or duck-bill, which grew to 43 ft (13 m) long. Plant fossils have been found with some hadrosaur skeletons, which suggests a diet of trees and shrubs. Hadrosaurs laid eggs in nests. A colony of hadrosaur nests was found grouped together in Montana, indicating these creatures lived in herds.

Edmontosaurus

Elongated shape

Rare egg

Fragments of broken dinosaur eggs are quite common, but complete eggs are rare. This *Oviraptor* egg was found in Mongolia in the 1920s and was part of the first evidence that dinosaurs laid eggs.

Powerful teeth for crushing vegetation

Sharp beak for cutting plants

Skull of Edmontosaurus

Knee bones

Dinosaurs varied in size. One of the largest, *Brachiosaurus*, weighed 60 tons—as much as 14 elephants—while the smallest was the size of a chicken. This image shows a femur (upper leg bone) of a *Hypsilophodon*, 4 in (10 cm) in length, compared to the same bone of an *Apatosaurus*, which is 6 ft 6 in (2 m) long.

Hypsilophodon *femur*

Apatosaurus *femur*

Tyrannosaurus *used its strong skull to crash into prey.*

Monster-stalking
Some people still search in vain for living examples of dinosaurs.

Tyrannosaurus

Fleet of foot
The Cretaceous dinosaur *Hypsilophodon* grew to 6 ft 6 in 2 m) long. It was probably agile and fast.

Large holes, or fenestrae, helped lighten the weight of the skull.

Skull of *Tyrannosaurus*

Sharp, pointed teeth— up to 7 in (18 cm) long

Dinosaur king
One of the most famous dinosaurs is *Tyrannosaurus*. This was among the largest meat-eating animals ever on land. It was 39 ft (12 m) long from head to tail. The sharp, pointed teeth, seen in this skull, show it was a meat-eater.

Dinosaur discovery

The first descriptions of dinosaur fossil bones were made 200 years ago. Teeth and bones of *Iguanodon* were found in England by Gideon and Mary Mantell. Bones of *Megalosaurus* and *Hylaeosaurus* were later discovered. In 1841, British anatomist Sir Richard Owen coined the name dinosaur, meaning "terrible lizard." Huge numbers of dinosaur remains were found in North America in the 19th century, while other finds were made in Tanzania, China, Mongolia, and Argentina. Every other week a new dinosaur species is discovered.

Mantell's tooth

This is one of the original *Iguanodon* teeth named by Gideon Mantell in 1825.

Mantell's quarry

Gideon Mantell was a doctor and fossil collector. The *Iguanodon* teeth and bones he described came from a quarry in Cuckfield, England, where rocks of the early Cretaceous age were dug up for use as gravel.

Big reptile

In 1824, British geologist and paleontologist William Buckland discovered dinosaur bones at Stonesfield in Oxfordshire, England. He called the animal *Megalosaurus*, which means "big lizard." This jaw bone belonged to a *Megalosaurus* and comes from the same area as Buckland's specimens.

Large head carried on a short, muscular neck

Big and bigger

Megalosaurus was a Jurassic meat-eater related to the larger and better known *Tyrannosaurus*.

👁 EYEWITNESS

Bolortsetseg Minjin
Mongolian paleontologist Bolortsetseg Minjin is known for her research on dinosaurs from the Gobi Desert, an important site for fossil excavations. She has also been active in repatriating fossils illegally removed from Mongolia, such as this skull of a juvenile *Tarbosaurus*.

1 Extracting dinosaur bones
Paleontologists remove rock from around the fossil. Once it is exposed enough, they may try to identify it.

2 Protecting bones
The bones can be fragile. They are protected in a plaster jacket made by wrapping them in scrim (open-weave fabric) soaked in plaster of Paris.

3 Removing the bones
Once they are marked for identification, the bones are removed from the site and taken to a laboratory for preparation. Large bones still embedded in rock may require a pulley.

Claws
Amateur collector Bill Walker found this claw bone in a claypit in Surrey, England. The Natural History Museum in London realized its importance and excavated more bones. Nicknamed "Claws," this dinosaur was named *Baryonyx walkeri* to honour its discoverer.

Claw find
Bill Walker with the claw bone of *Baryonyx,* which he discovered in 1983.

Upper arm

Toe bones

Fish-eater
Baryonyx was an unusual dinosaur because it ate fish. Its head was shaped like a fish-eating crocodile.

Wing support

This long finger bone supported the wing of a *Pteranodon*, one of the largest flying animals.

Winged wonders

Insects were the first animals to fly more than 300 million years ago. Flying vertebrates appeared almost 100 million years later. Flapping flight evolved in three groups of vertebrates: extinct pterosaurs, birds, and bats. Pterosaurs were reptiles related to dinosaurs, with a long fourth finger to support the wing. Bird wings are supported by the fingers and forearm. Bats have wings supported by four fingers. Bones of flying vertebrates are light and fragile, so they are rarely fossilized.

Well balanced

Pteranodon (above) was a pterosaur with a bony crest on its head that counterbalanced its long toothless beak. It was a fish-eater that flew over the sea like the modern albatross.

Body covered by fine fur

Toothed beak

Furry reptile

The small Jurassic pterosaur *Pterodactylus* had membranous wings, claws, and a furry body. Evidence for fur comes from pterosaurs found in Kazakhstan with hairlike impressions around the body. This suggests that pterosaurs were warm-blooded and used fur as insulation. Pterosaurs appeared in the Triassic Period and were extinct by the end of the Cretaceous Period.

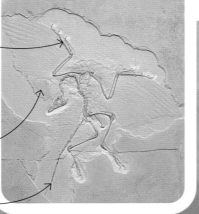

Claws

Impression of feathers like a bird's

Bony tail like a reptile's

Ancient bird

Archaeopteryx lived 150 million years ago. Specimens are considered the world's most precious fossils. Only 11 more have been found since this first one was discovered in 1861. It is now on display in the Natural History Museum in Berlin.

Archaeopteryx fossil

Enormous egg

The Madagascan elephant bird *Aepyornis maximus* was 6 ft 6 in (2 m) tall. Its fossil eggs are the largest birds' eggs known, measuring around 13 in (34 cm) in length. In comparison, an ostrich egg—the largest egg of a modern bird—measures only 6 in (15 cm).

Elephant bird

Flying mammal

Bats are mammals. They date back to the Eocene Epoch. As they roost in caves, their fossil bones can often be found in cave deposits.

Rare find

Feathers are seldom fossilized. Occasionally they are found in fine-grained sediments such as this Oligocene limestone.

Fossil feather

Modern bird's feather

Ostrich

Ostrich egg

Elephant bird egg

Clawed fingers like a reptile's

Mistaken identity

Scientists first believed that *Compsognathus* was an ancestor of birds. In 1973, German experts found that a specimen identified as *Compsognathus* was actually *Archaeopteryx*! While they were both small animals, only *Archaeopteryx* could fly.

Compsognathus

Fine skull

Fossilized bird remains are rare. This Eocene skull comes from the bird *Prophaethon*.

Reconstruction of an *Archaeopteryx*

Mammal variety

Animals as varied as mice, elephants, kangaroos, bats, cats, whales, and humans are all mammals. They are warm-blooded and produce milk to suckle their infants. Most give birth to live young, have hairy skins, complex teeth, and are highly active. The first mammals appeared at the same time as the earliest dinosaurs, in the Triassic Period. Nearly all Mesozoic mammals were small shrew-like animals, but in the Cenozoic Era, they diversified into the many types we know today. Complete fossil mammals are rare—many species are known only from their teeth.

Ice-Age mammal
Mammoths were elephant-like mammals adapted to life in cold climates during the Pleistocene Ice Ages. Some skeletons have been found preserved in permafrost.

Rodents
Rodents include rats, mice, and squirrels. Their large, chisel-like incisor teeth grow continuously. Rodents date from Paleocene times. This is *Ischyromys* from the famous Oligocene mammal beds of the White River Badlands in the US.

Skull of *Ischyromys*

Meat-eaters
Carnivorous mammals have large canine teeth. These were developed to their greatest extent in the upper jaws of the sabretooths. They may have used their long teeth to stab their prey. This skull is *Smilodon* from the Pleistocene Epoch.

Skull of *Smilodon*

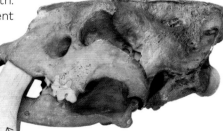

Large canine tooth

Smilodon

Grinding tooth
Massive mammoths needed to eat large quantities of vegetation. Their huge high-crowned cheek teeth, like this one, had ridges of hard enamel to grind up vegetation.

Ridges of hard enamel

Thick fur to protect from cold

Fruit-eaters

Monkeys, apes, and humans belong to a group of mammals called primates. Many primates are omnivores and so have a mixed diet, but some eat mostly fruit. This skull of the Miocene ape _Proconsul_ has blunt teeth typical of fruit-eaters. As fruit is poor in protein, _Proconsul_ may have supplemented its diet with leaves from the trees.

Skull of _Proconsul_

Long tusks for defense

Blunt teeth typical of a fruit-eater

Fish-eaters

Potamotherium lived in freshwater lakes in the early Miocene Epoch and fed on fish. It was similar to a modern otter but was better adapted to life in water. It may have been a forerunner of seals, which first became common in the sea during the late Miocene.

Skull of _Potamotherium_

Plant-eaters

Many herbivorous mammals have cheek teeth capable of withstanding wear caused by constant chewing. Browsers eat mostly leaves, while grazers mostly eat grass. _Cainotherium_ was a rabbit-like browser whose closest, but distant, living relative is a camel.

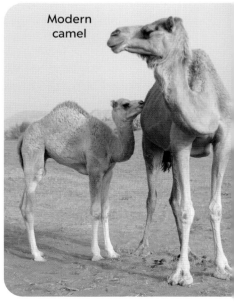

Modern camel

Skull of _Cainotherium_

A world apart

The geological record shows Australia's isolation for 60 million years, when plate movements caused the landmass to start to drift away from Antarctica. This is why many native mammals in Australia are unique. Marsupials differ from other mammals in that they have pouches where the young are reared after birth. The fleshy pouches do not fossilize, but features of the bones and teeth distinguish marsupial fossils from those of placentals. There are still many species of pouched mammal in Australia, including the kangaroo and koala.

Hip bone connecting the leg to the spine

Two front teeth

This skeleton of the extinct marsupial *Diprotodon* is about 10 ft (3 m) long. Its name, meaning "two front teeth," refers to the large, rodentlike incisors used for cropping vegetation. The pair of epipubic bones in the pelvic area can be used to distinguish pouched from placental mammals. *Diprotodon* comes from Pleistocene rocks and may have been hunted by First Australians—some animals in their paintings could be *Diprotodon*.

Epipubic bones helped support the pouch.

Drifting landmasses

These two maps show the position of Australia about 60 million years ago and 45 million years ago, after the split from Antarctica. The isolation of Australia prevented its colonization by placental mammals, apart from some bats and rodents. These might otherwise have replaced the native animals. This is probably what happened to the marsupials of South America, such as the extinct sabretooth *Thylacosmilus*, when placental mammals invaded South America after North and South America were joined.

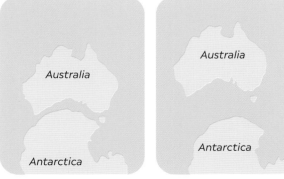

Australia	Australia
Antarctica	Antarctica
60 million years ago	**45 million years ago**

Giant wombat?

Diprotodon was a herbivore. It probably looked like a long-legged wombat.

56

Spine, the main support for the body

Rodentlike incisors for cropping vegetation

Blunt teeth for grinding vegetation

Rib cage that protected the heart and lungs

A fake?

When platypus remains were brought to London in the 18th century, they were dismissed as fake! The platypus has fur, webbed feet, and a beak. It is not a marsupial but a monotreme (meaning "one hole") mammal.

Australian outback

The climate of Australia in the Pliocene Epoch became drier, and grasslands spread at the expense of forests. The Australian outback is now dry and inhospitable, but many native species of mammals thrive there.

ALIKE BUT DIFFERENT

A feature of mammal evolution is that for many placental mammals there is an equivalent pouched mammal in Australia. This parallel evolution occurred as animals adapted to similar ways of life.

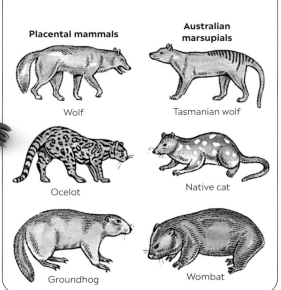

Placental mammals	Australian marsupials
Wolf	Tasmanian wolf
Ocelot	Native cat
Groundhog	Wombat

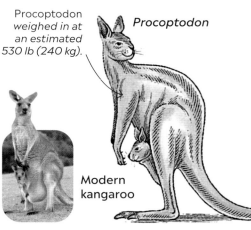

Procoptodon weighed in at an estimated 530 lb (240 kg).

Procoptodon

Modern kangaroo

Giant kangaroo

Large grazing kangaroos were common in the Pliocene. A kangaroo of the Pleistocene Epoch, *Procoptodon* was 10 ft (3 m) tall! A modern kangaroo reaches 6–7 ft (2 m) when extended to its full height.

Human fossils

Fossils of people (hominids) are rare and fragmentary. They teach us about the origin and development of modern people. The story begins with the apelike *Ardipithecus* and *Australopithecus*, and ends with *Homo sapiens*. The nearest living relatives of humans are the African Great Apes (chimpanzees and bonobos), but humans have a larger brain and walk on two legs rather than four. Fossil hominids reveal how differences evolved over time.

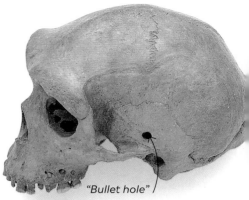

"Bullet hole"

Alien shot

This skull from Zambia is an early species of *Homo*. One writer claimed the hole was made by a bullet shot by an alien 120,000 years ago! In fact, it was made by an abscess.

First steps

These fossil footprints in Tanzania came from two-footed hominids. They were probably two adults and a child *Australopithecus* walking over damp volcanic ash. The ash hardened and was buried under more ash and sediment. They prove that a species of primate walked on two feet at least 3.6 million years ago.

Child's footprint

Comparing features

These skulls of a human and a chimpanzee look similar, but there are differences. Humans have larger brains. The average volume of a human's brain is 1,400 cm³, but a chimp's brain is 400 cm³. The domed human cranium can house a bigger brain. The teeth are different. A chimp cannot move its jaws side to side when chewing as its canine teeth overlap.

Chimpanzee skull

Human skull

Antler art

This sculpted antler is 12,000 years old and shows a male reindeer following a female. It was carved using simple flint tools. This shows the development of art and culture that is unique to humans.

Carved reindeer

Using a stone
to chip off flakes

Pebble tool

Flint
hand ax

The oldest tools

Human beings are described as toolmakers. This pebble tool is an early stone tool made by *Homo habilis* ("handy man") nearly 2 million years ago.

Southern ape

Several *Australopithecus* ("southern ape") species lived in Africa between about 4.5 and 1.5 million years ago. Some were heavily built with bony skull crests. Others were lightly built, like this South African example.

Louis Leakey

The oldest hominids have been found in South and East Africa. Kenyan British archaeologist Louis Leakey is known for his finds of *Australopithecus*.

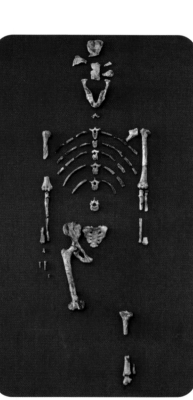

Lucy

This adult female skeleton of *Australopithecus* was discovered in 1974.

Upright man

Homo erectus ("upright man") has been found in Africa and South East Asia. It lived between 2 million and 100,000 years ago. The cranium size indicates a brain bigger than *Australopithecus* but smaller than modern humans.

Carved animal head

Sickle

Arrowheads

Harpoon

Sharp flint pieces

Hunting tools

This 10,000-year-old sickle is made of goat horn with sharp pieces of flint forming a cutting edge. The barbed harpoon next to it was carved from an antler. The 4,000-year-old arrowheads on the top right are made of flint, a flaky rock used by early people.

Rock painting

These animal paintings were made by early people living in what is now Algeria.

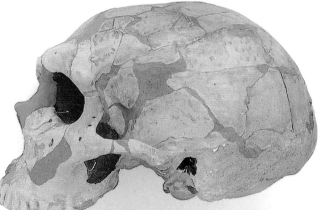

Ice-age relative

Neanderthals lived in Europe and western Asia before and during the last Ice Age, between 400,000 and 30,000 years ago. They were given the name because the first specimen was found in a cave in the Neander Valley, Germany. Today they are classed as a distinct species, *Homo neanderthalensis*.

Living fossils

Fossils show us that animals and plants have change enormously since life on Earth began. Some have changed so much that modern species are very different from their fossil ancestors. There are also animals and plants living today that are almost identical to ancient fossils. The most striking examples of these "living fossils" are those animals and plants that are rare nowadays, such as the coelacanth and slit shells, and which were known as fossils before they were discovered to be still living.

Modern horseshoe crab

Tuatara have no external ears, but they are sensitive to vibrations.

Sole survivor

The tuatara is the only survivor of a group of reptiles dating back to the Triassic. It inhabits a few islands off the mainland of New Zealand.

Modern *Ginkgo* branch

Fossil *Ginkgo*

Lone ranger

Ginkgos first appeared in the Permian and were more widespread in the past than they are today. Only a single species, *Ginkgo biloba*, lives today (above). Known as the maidenhair tree, it grows in western China. The fan-shaped leaves are easily recognizable when fossilized, as in this Jurassic example (left).

Presumed dead

The most famous of all living fossils is the coelacanth, which ranges back to the Devonian. It was thought to be extinct until a living one was caught off the South African coast in 1938. Some have been photographed alive off the Comoro Islands, northeast of Madagascar. In 1998, a new species of coelacanth was found off the Indonesian coast.

Fossil coelacanth

False crabs

These are not true crabs but are related to spiders and scorpions. The modern horseshoe crab, *Limulus*, (left) lives near shorelines in the Far East and along the Atlantic Ocean off North America. It is similar to *Mesolimulus*, (right) a fossil from 150 million years ago.

Fossil horseshoe crab

Fossil slit shell

Modern Virginia opossum

Modern slit shell

Back to life

Snails related to *Pleurotomaria*, the slit shells, are rare today. Living examples were first discovered in 1856 at sea depths of more than 650 ft (200 m). Almost identical shells had long been known as fossils.

Variety of teeth indicating a mixed diet

Fossil skull of a didelphid

Ancient mammal

Didelphids, including the opossums, are pouched mammals from the Americas. Didelphids are closely related to some fossil animals from the Mesozoic. Their fossil records show numerous similarities with modern didelphid features.

Wanted!

The first modern coelacanth was identified in 1938 by Professor J. L. B. Smith in South Africa. He offered a reward for a second one, which he received in 1952.

Commemorative stamps from the Comoro Islands

Modern coelacanth

Wedgwood plate commemorating the catching of a live coelacanth

Fossil hunting

Fossil collecting is a hobby that requires only basic tools. Sea cliffs, quarries, and other rock exposures provide productive places for fossil collectors. It may be necessary to get permission to collect from land owners, and overcollecting in one area is best avoided.

Field notebook
Rock formations and locality of finds should be recorded in a field notebook.

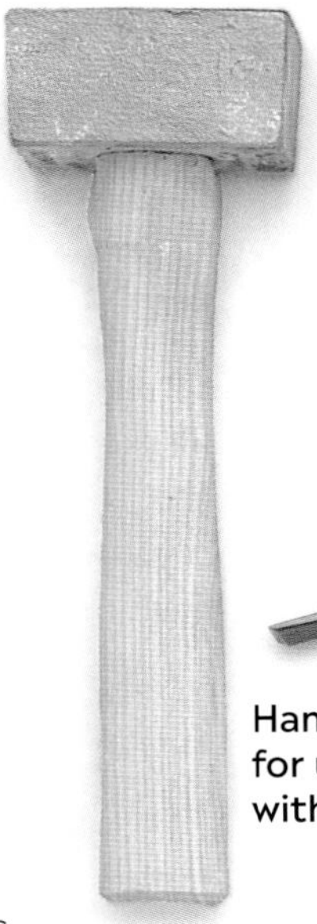

Chisels
A hammer and chisel can help extract fossils from their matrix (surrounding rock).

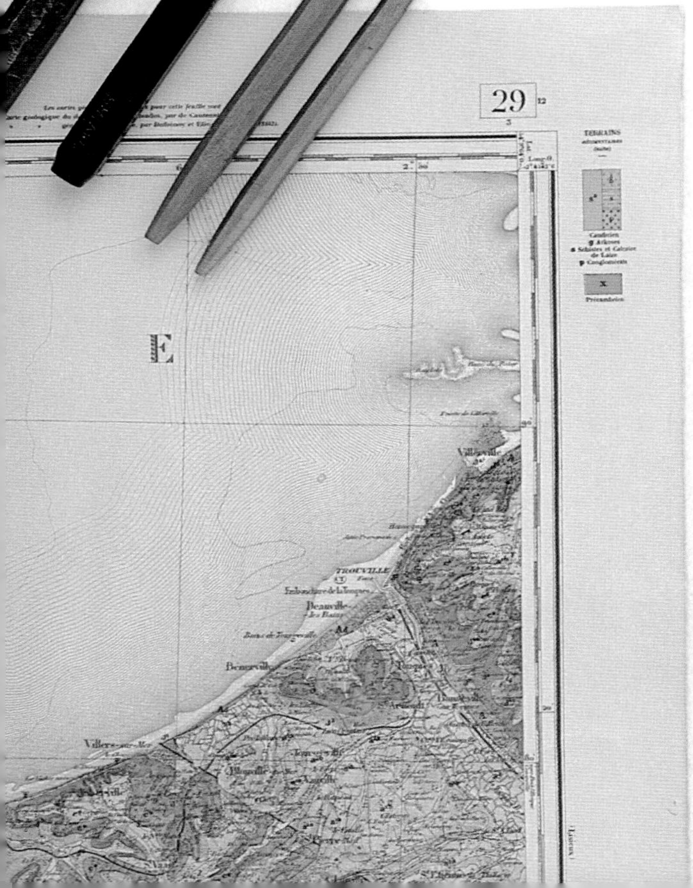

Hammer for use with a chisel

Hammers
A geological hammer can be used to break up rocks.

Trowels
Fossils in soft sediment can be removed using a trowel.

Standard geological hammer

Fossil map
Geological maps help locate promising places to collect fossils, as they identify the names and ages of rocks.

Brushes
These brushes can remove sediment during excavation of fossils from soft rocks.

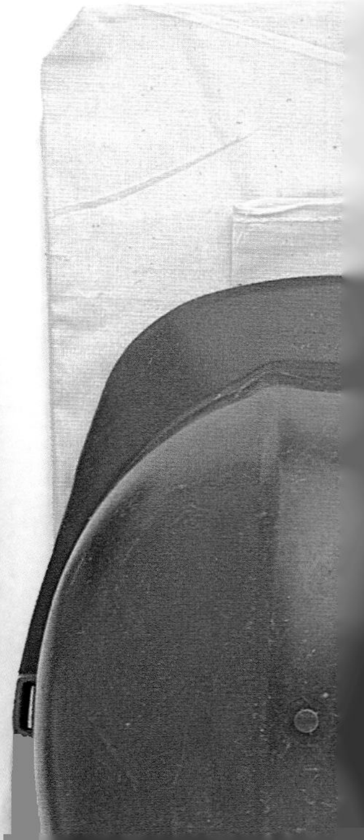

Safety helmet

29

Sieve for separating out small fossils

Drawer of specimens

After cleaning with water, fossils should be stored with care. Cardboard trays are good for holding labeled fossils.

Bivalve

Brachiopod

Echinoid

Coral

Echinoid

Ammonite

Hand lens

A pocket hand lens with a magnification of 10 to 20 times is valuable for examining fossils in the field.

Microscope slides

Small fossils can be kept in wooden or cardboard cavity slides, so they can be looked at under a microscope. They should be stuck down or secured beneath a transparent glass cover.

Close study

A magnifying glass or a binocular microscope is best for close study.

Brachiopod
Sphaeroidothyris sphaeroidalis

Jurassic. Bajocian Upper Inferior Oolite East Cliff, Burbon Bradstock, Dorset, England

Labels

Labeling fossil specimens is essential, including the rock formation and location. Fossils can be numbered with sticky labels.

Canvas bag for larger fossils

Plastic pots for collecting small fossils

Goggles

Drawings

Drawings enhance fossil collections. These books were compiled over a century ago.

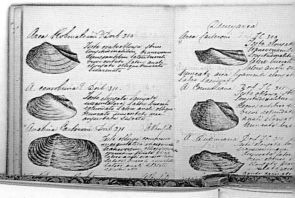

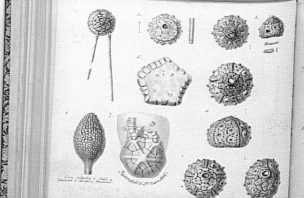

Did you **know?**

AMAZING FACTS

Dromaeosaur fossil

In the 1990s, paleontologists began to dig up fossils of feathered dinosaurs in China—the best evidence yet that birds evolved from dinosaurs. Dromaeosaurs were small, fast-moving meat-eaters that had primitive feathers.

RECORD BREAKERS

 Earliest fossil embryo
The earliest-known fossilized animal embryo dates back 670 million years in Guizhou province, China.

 Oldest fossil flower
A 125-million-year-old flowering plant, named *Archaefructus liaoningensis*, was found in Liaoning province, China, in 1998.

 Largest-ever land mammal
An 2 ft 9 in (83 cm) long skull fossil in Mongolia belonged to *Andrewsarchus*, an Eocene carnivore. It could have been 19 ft (6 m) long and weighed a ton.

 Oldest fossil fish
Two fish, *Haikouichthys ercaicunensis* and *Myllokunmingia fengjiaoa*, were found in rocks from 530 million years ago in Yunnan, China.

The first fossils of the arthropod *Anomalocaris* were limbs, jaws, or other body parts. The huge front limbs were thought to be tails from an extinct shrimp. It was only when a complete fossil was found that scientists put together this creature.

Anomodonts are the most primitive beasts with mammal characteristics that we know. The 260-million-year-old skull of one was found in South Africa in 1999. About the size of sheep, anomodonts were plant-eaters that lived long before the dinosaurs. They had some reptilian characteristics, and some mammalian.

Opalized shell

Fossils of an Eocene whale, *Ambulocetus*, show that it was about 10 ft (3 m) long and looked like a big, furry crocodile! Although it had the teeth and skull of a whale and was an excellent swimmer, it also had legs for walking on land. Its name means "walking whale."

Fossilized insect and spider in amber

In the *Jurassic Park* movies, DNA from the bodies of insects fossilized in amber was used to reconstruct whole herds of dinosaurs. Scientists have extracted DNA in this way, but only fragments of it—not enough to rebuild prehistoric animals.

At Holzmaden, Germany, there are fossils of thousands of Jurassic marine creatures. One amazing fossil is an ichthyosaur in the act of giving birth.

Australia has large opal deposits that formed in the early Cretaceous Period. During mining for opal gems, specimens of opalized shells (left) have been found. One of the finest opal fossils is "Eric," a complete pliosaur skeleton (below). Pliosaurs are a type of plesiosaur that lived in seas of the Jurassic and Cretaceous periods.

A complete Pleistocene animal was excavated in 1999 by French paleontologist Bernard Buigues. The Siberian woolly mammoth had lain frozen for over 20,000 years. It was named "Jarkov," after the family who discovered it.

"Eric", the opalized pliosaur

QUESTIONS AND ANSWERS

Where are the oldest animal fossils on Earth?

Burgess Shale in British Columbia, Canada, used to be the best site for Cambrian fossils, but now older finds are coming out of sites near Kunming, in the province of Yunnan, southwest China. Preserved in rock known as the Maotianshan Shales, they include the earliest examples of fish to be discovered. Thousands of near-perfect soft-bodied fossils have been found. Collectively, they are known as the "Chengjiang fauna," after a village near the sites.

Where in the world is the Petrified Forest?

The Petrified Forest is a collection of fossilized logs and tree trunks in an area of national park in the Arizona desert. The trees date back nearly 220 million years. As well as plants, there are about 40 fossilized bee nests, the earliest ever found, and lots of bone fragments from vertebrates, including dinosaurs, pterosaurs, fish, primitive reptiles, and amphibians.

Fossilized sections of tree trunk in the Petrified Forest, Arizona

Pederpes finneyae

Which animal was first to walk on land?

The earliest fossil evidence is the skeleton of a 3 ft (1 m) long amphibian, *Pederpes finneyae*, that lived 345 million years ago. All the earlier feet fossils that have been found were designed to point back, and would have been used for swimming. *Pederpes'* ankle joints were evolved to take steps forward. *Pederpes* probably spent some time on land and some in the water. It lived in swamps in what is now Scotland.

Which North American river is stocked full of fossilized fish?

The world's richest fish fossil site is the Green River Formation at Fossil Butte National Monument, Wyoming, which covers an area of 25,000 sq miles (64,750 sq km). The fossils date back some 55 million years to the Eocene Epoch, when there was a series of large inland lakes on the site. The dead animals and plants that sank to the bottom of these lakes have been exquisitely preserved. Thousands of fish specimens have been found, as well as turtles, birds, mammals, and crocodiles.

How many bones are there in a dinosaur?

Dinosaurs have about 200 separate bones on average, although the exact number depends on the species. We have discovered the complete skeletons of very few species of dinosaurs. In some species, just a single bone has been found and the shapes of the others must be figured out by comparison with related species.

A dig in Yunnan province, China

Diplomystus dentatus, or herring, from the Green River Formation

Identifying fossils

Fossils can be split into three groups—plants, animals with backbones (vertebrates), and animals without backbones (invertebrates). There are also trace fossils, such as animal tracks and droppings.

Fossil id
These illustrations are from a book that identifies invertebrate fossil finds. It was published by the British Museum (Natural History) in 1907.

PLANT FOSSILS

Tree trunk
Whole forests of preserved tree trunks have been found fossilized, with the growth rings visible and intact.

Sequoia cone
This ironstone fossil is a pine cone from a sequoia tree. The oldest sequoia fossils date to Jurassic times.

Club moss
This club moss fossil is *Archaeosigillaria* from the Carboniferous Period. Once as tall as trees, they are now small plants.

Fern
This fern leaf was found in the Permian Hermit Shale. Fossilized plant parts can be found in shales and mudstones.

ANIMAL FOSSILS: VERTEBRATES

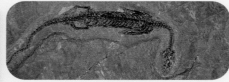

Reptile
This skeleton is of *Pachypleurosaurus*, a swimming reptile that lived in what is now Europe, in the Triassic Period.

Fish
This freshwater perch, *Priscacara*, was found in the fossil-rich Green River Formation.

Bird
One of the world's most famous fossils, this is *Archaeopteryx*, the oldest-known bird, in limestone.

Mammal
This fossil of *Macrocranion*, an Eocene hedgehog, was found at Grube Messel, Germany.

Teeth
The vertebrate fossils that amateur hunters are most likely to find are teeth, especially shark teeth.

Belemnite
Belemnites were mollusks related to modern-day squid and octopus. All that is left is the animal's internal shell.

Trilobite
Encrinurus lived in shallow seas in the Silurian Period. The pimpled head gave it the nickname "strawberry-headed trilobite."

Crinoid (sea lily)
Crinoids were common in the Paleozoic seas. *Cupressocrinites* used its petal-like arms to filter food from the sea water.

Brachiopod
About 0.75 in (2 cm) long, this brachiopod is *Goniorhynchia*, which lived in the Middle Jurassic Period.

Ammonite
Gunnarites is a Late Cretaceous ammonite with a distinctive coiled shell.

Foraminifera (microfossil)
This highly-magnified image shows the fossilized skeleton of the tiny, single-celled protozoa *Elphidium*.

Bivalve
About 2.75 in (7 cm) long, this Jurassic oyster, called *Gryphaea*, is more popularly known as the Devil's toenail.

Coral
Colpophyllia is often called "brain coral" because of the patterning on the surface of the colony.

Gastropod
This snail is *Pleurotomaria*, a slit shell, with distinctive knobbly riblets. A living relative is seen on p.61.

Sponge
Early Cretaceous sponge, *Raphidonema farringdonense*, was common in shallow seas in what is now Oxfordshire, England.

Graptolite
These are *Rhabdinopora*, the earliest graptolite. Graptolites were colonial planktonic animals.

Echinoid (sea urchin)
This fossil urchin, *Phymosoma*, lived in the Cretaceous Period. Its test (skeleton) and spines have been fossilized in chalk.

Find out **more**

To find out more about fossils, go to local or national museums and see some spectacular collections. You could look out for television programs about fossil hunters and their exciting new finds. Visit a library or fossil websites to read up more. You could also become a fossil hunter. It is a good idea to join a local club. Fossil collecting is great fun, and you will soon build up your own collection.

Paleontologists in the lab

In this French laboratory, experts are removing fossilized bones from a plaster jacket. The plaster was set around the fossils at the place they were discovered to protect them during transportation.

Amateur fossil hunter

It takes a great deal of patience to be a fossil hunter. Quite often, you might come home empty-handed, so it is important to enjoy the quest for its own sake. This fossil hunter in Florida is sifting through shingle, a method suitable only for certain beaches.

Paleontologist at work

Dinosaur National Monument in Colorado, is a protected site. Its fossilized dinosaur bones are dug out by professionals. If you want a career as a paleontologist, aim for a science degree and gather experience on digs.

Jet necklace

See how many "fossils" you can spot in a day. Amber and jet are just fossilized plant matter. Think about fossil fuels and their by-products.

USEFUL WEBSITES

- Links to natural history museums around the world
  www.ucmp.berkeley.edu/subway/nathistmus.html
- America's National Museum of Natural History
  naturalhistory.si.edu
- Natural History Museum, London
  www.nhm.ac.uk
- Link to DK's interactive website on paleontology and fossils
  www.dkfindout.com/us/dinosaurs-and-prehistoric-life/fossils/

National Museum of Natural History

The fossil gallery at the National Museum of Natural History in Washington, DC, (below) takes visitors back in geological time, using fossils to show how life on our planet has changed dramatically. Highlights include two mounted skeletons showing a *Tyrannosaurus* devouring a *Triceratops*.

The Cambridge Museum

Founded in 1814, the University Museum of Zoology in Cambridge, England, (below) houses a superb collection of fossils. It includes fish from Canada and Scotland, mammals from North America, and reptiles from Africa.

Dinosaur museum

Europe's first museum dedicated to dinosaurs opened at Espéraza in France, in 1992. Many displays are fossils dug from Late Cretaceous rock deposits. The collection includes bones and eggs, like these of the titanosaur.

PLACES TO VISIT

AMERICAN MUSEUM OF NATURAL HISTORY, NEW YORK, US
The largest collection of vertebrate fossils.
• *Buettneria*, an early four-limbed animal
• Reconstructions of *T. rex* and *Apatosaurus*

MUSEUM NATIONAL D'HISTOIRE NATURELLE, PARIS, FRANCE
A leading natural history museum.
• Gallery of specimens that chart the evolution of the vertebrate skeleton
• The world's oldest fossilized insects
• Excellent collection of plant fossils

NATIONAL MUSEUM OF NATURAL HISTORY, WASHINGTON, DC, US
A big collection of Burgess Shale fossils.
• Forty dinosaurs on display
• A collection of over 200,000 foraminifera

THE NATURAL HISTORY MUSEUM, LONDON, ENGLAND
Attractions to look out for include:
• Gallery of dinosaurs
• "From the Beginning" exhibition of ancient life

Natural History Museum, London

The Natural History Museum (left) contains over 80 million specimens that span 4.6 billion years, from the formation of the solar system to the present day.

Glossary

Devonian fish

Anthracite

AMBER
Fossilized resin of an ancient conifer.

AMMONITE
An extinct cephalopod with a shell, common in the Mesozoic Era.

AMPHIBIAN
A cold-blooded animal adapted to life on land and in water.

ANATOMIST
Someone who studies the structure of animals.

ANGIOSPERM
A flowering plant that protects its seeds inside a fruit.

ANTHRACITE
Hard, shiny, jet-black coal.

ARTHROPOD
An animal with jointed legs, a segmented body, and an exoskeleton, such as a trilobite.

BACTERIUM
A tiny living organism, usually consisting of a single cell.

BELEMNITE
Extinct cephalopod related to the modern-day squid.

Diplomystus, a herring relative, from the Early Eocene

Eocene angiosperm

BIVALVE
A mollusk with two shells that are generally mirror images.

BRACHIOPOD
An animal with two shells, one slightly larger than the other.

CAMBRIAN
The geological period from 539–485 MYA.

CARBONIFEROUS
The geological period from 359–299 MYA.

CARNIVORE
An animal that eats other animals.

CENOZOIC
Our present geological era, which began 66 MYA—the age of mammals.

CEPHALOPOD
A mollusk with tentacles or arms.

COAL MEASURE FOREST
Swampy forest where plant matter from the Carboniferous Period turned into coal over time.

CONCRETION
A mineral mass that forms around an object such as a shell or a bone.

COPROLITE
Fossilized animal dropping.

CORAL
A colony or group of tiny marine animals called polyps that have hard outer skeletons.

CRETACEOUS
The last geological period of the Mesozoic, from 145–66 MYA.

CRUST
The thin outer layer of Earth.

CRUSTACEAN
An arthropod with a hard shell, jointed legs, and compound eyes.

DENDRITE
A branched crystal growth resembling a plant.

DEVONIAN
The geological period from 419–359 MYA.

ECHINODERM
A marine animal with five-point symmetry.

ELEMENT
Material that cannot be made into more simple substances by chemical means.

EOCENE
The geological period from 56–34 MYA.

EROSION
The wearing away of rock by wind, water, and ice.

EVOLUTION
The process by which species change into new ones over multiple generations.

EXOSKELETON
Tough outer casing that protects the body of some invertebrates.

FOSSIL
The naturally preserved remains of animals or plants, or evidence of their activities.

FOSSIL FUEL
Materials formed from the remains of ancient living things, that can be burned to give off energy, such as oil and coal.

GEOLOGY
The study of Earth, including rocks.

GYMNOSPERM
A plant that produces seeds in a cone.

HERBIVORE
An animal that eats plants.

HOLOCENE
Our present geological epoch, which began around 10,000 years ago.

ICHTHYOSAUR
A Mesozoic swimming reptile.

IGNEOUS ROCK
Rock formed by cooling of molten magma.

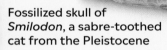

Fossilized skull of *Smilodon*, a sabre-toothed cat from the Pleistocene

IMPERVIOUS
Rock that liquid cannot penetrate.

INVERTEBRATE
An animal without a backbone.

JURASSIC
The geological period from 210–145 MYA.

LIMESTONE
A calcareous sedimentary rock often made of the fossilized remains of shelled creatures.

LYCOPOD
The club mosses, a group of primitive plants that reproduce by spores.

MAMMAL
A warm-blooded, hair-covered animal that usually suckles its young.

MESOZOIC
The geological era from 252–66 MYA, known as the age of the dinosaurs.

METAMORPHIC ROCK
Rock that forms due to heat, pressure, or a combination.

MIOCENE
The geological epoch from 23–5 MYA.

MOLLUSK
A type of unsegmented invertebrate.

NATURALIST
Someone who studies nature.

OLIGOCENE
The geological epoch from 34–23 MYA.

ORDOVICIAN
The geological period from 485–444 MYA.

PALEOCENE
The first geological epoch of the Cenozoic, from 66–56 MYA.

PALEONTOLOGY
The study of fossils.

PALEOZOIC
The geological era from 539–252 MYA.

PANGAEA
The supercontinent that formed in the Late Paleozoic.

PERMIAN
The last geological period of the Paleozoic, from 299–252 MYA.

PLACODERM
An extinct fish with armour and jaws.

PLACENTAL
A mammal whose young develop inside the mother's body and are nourished by an organ called the placenta.

PLEISTOCENE
The geological epoch from 2.6–0.01 MYA, including the last Ice Ages.

PLESIOSAUR
An extinct, long-necked marine reptile.

PLIOCENE
The geological epoch from 5–2.6 MYA.

PRECAMBRIAN
The earliest geological interval, from 4,600 MYA, when Earth formed, until 539 MYA.

The tests (skeletons) of a fossilized heart urchin, left, and a modern sea urchin, below

PTEROSAUR
An extinct flying reptile.

REPTILE
A cold-blooded, scaly animal that usually lays eggs.

ROCK
Solid mixtures of minerals.

SEDIMENTARY ROCK
Rock that forms at Earth's surface from rock fragments and other deposited substances.

SHALE
A rock made of compacted clay.

SILURIAN
The geological period from 444–419 MYA.

TEST
An echinoid's plated skeleton.

TRACE FOSSIL
Fossilized evidence of the activities of an animal, such as footprints.

TRIASSIC
The first geological period of the Mesozoic, from 252–201 MYA.

VERTEBRATE
An animal with a backbone.

A sea sponge from the Cretaceous Period

Index

Acknowledgments

The publisher would like to thank the following people for their help with making the book: Plymouth Marine Laboratory, National Museum of Wales, Kew Gardens for specimens for photography; Lester Cheeseman and Thomas Keenes for additional design assistance; Arpit Aggarwal and Anna Kunst for editorial assistance; Meryl Silbert; Karl Shone for additional photography (pp.18–19); Saloni Singh for the jacket; Hazel Beynon for proofreading; and Elizabeth Wise for the index.

The author would like to thank: M. K. Howarth; C. Patterson; R. A. Fortey; C. H. C. Brunton; A. W. Gentry; B. R. Rosen; J. B. Richardson; P. L. Forey; N. J. Morris; C. B. Stringer; A. B. Smith; J. E. P. Whittaker; R. Croucher; S. F. Morris; C. R. Hill; A. C. Milner; R. L. Hodgkinson; C. A. Walker; R. J. Cleevely; C. H. Shute; V. T. Young; D. N. Lewis; A. E. Longbottom; M. Crawley; R. Kruszynski; C. Bell; S. C. Naylor; A. Lum; R. W. Ingle; P. D. Jenkins; P. D. Hillyard; D. T. Moore; J. W. Schopf; C. M. Butler; P. W. Jackson

The publisher would like to thank the following for their kind permission to reproduce their images:
(a=above, b=below/bottom, c=center, f=far, l=left, r=right, t=top)

123RF.com: David Steele 55br; **Alamy Stock Photo:** Arcaid Images 28cla, Joe Belanger 31c, blickwinkel / B. Trapp 19tl, blickwinkel / McPHOTO / STR 19br, Dorling Kindersley ltd 33tr, Dotted Zebra 46cb, 52–53b, Florilegius 46bl, Peter Hermes Furian 7cb, Michele and Tom Grimm 21bl, Historic Collection 35br, Brian Jannsen 8–9t, Marion Kaplan 58bc, Natural History Museum, London 3tl, 5tr, 39tl, 50cra, 69cb, Nature Picture Library 43cla, Nature Picture Library / Chris & Monique Fallows 46ca, Nature Picture Library / Daniel Heuclin 43tl, Nature Picture Library / Konrad Wothe 44–45t, Nature Picture Library / Wild Wonders of Europe / Zankl 44cb, North Wind Picture Archives 12tr, Pictorial Press 47br, Enrico Della Pietra

20–21t, Lee Rentz 61ca, robertharding / Christina Gascoigne 21cb, Science History Images / Photo Researchers 1c, 6bc, 20bc, Witold Skrypczak 10tl, Aunt Spray 31crb, The History Collection 36tl, The Reading Room 66cla; **Aldus Archive:** 54br; **Ardea:** 9bl; **Biofotos/ Heather Angel:** 39br; **Booth Museum of Natural History:** 66bl; **Bridgeman Images:** 17l, Haldane Fine Art 14cl, Natural History Museum, London 51cra, 59c; **Dept. of Earth Sciences, University of Cambridge:** 39cr; **Bruce Coleman:** /Jeff Foote 39c, 40cl; **Simon Conway Morris:** 20br; **Corbis:** James L. Amos 65br, 68bl; **Dorling Kindersley:** Jon Hughes 21cb (Dinornis), 53tc, James Kuether 48c, Colin Keates / Natural History Museum 2br, Colin Keates / Natural History Museum, London 54cb, John Downes / Natural History Museum, London 50crb, Tim Parmenter / Natural History Museum 20cl, Gary Ombler / Senckenberg Gesellschaft Fuer Naturforschung Museum 49b, Gary Ombler, Oxford University Museum of Natural History 28tl, Harry Taylor Trustees of the National Museums Of Scotland 43br; **Dreamstime.com:** Daniel Eskridge 34–35c, Kjuuurs 57cb, Mickem 4tl, Witold Ryka 24cl, Michael Valos 28cra, Sara Winter 57cra; **Mary Evans Picture Library:** 13ml, 14tr, 20br; **Getty Images:** Scott Ferguson / 500px 25crb, Jonathan Blair / Corbis 59cla, Patrick AVENTURIER / Gamma-Rapho 51tc, David McNew 51tl, Moment / Highlywood Photography 38l, Newsmakers / Bobbie DeHerrera / Stringer 51tr, Roger Harris / Science Photo Library 49cla; **Getty Images / iStock:** E+ / cinoby 22–23b, GeorgiosArt 14bl, nattapon1975 41l; **Robert Harding Picture Library:** 29tc, 59b; **Mansell Collection:** 40b; **Adrienne Mayor:** Josiah Ober 16clb; **Bolortsetseg Minjin:** 50br; **Natural History Museum, London:** 66tr, 70c, 66tc, 66bc (below); / Geological Museum of China 64tl; **naturepl.com:** Ingo Arndt 42bl, Jane Burton 43ca, Fabio Liverani 42bc, MYN / Niall Benvie 44crb, Doug Wechsler 60–61c; **Trustees of the Natural History Museum, London:** 6–7c; **Oxford University Museum:**

66br (above), 71tc, 71b; **Planet Earth Pictures:** 63tc; **Rex Features:** Sipa Press 65c; **Ashok Sahni:** Taken from M R Sahni's personal photograph collection. 36bc; **Science Photo Library:** 58cl; James L. Amos 66cb, / Tony Craddock 65bl; Dorling Kindersley / UIG 33cr, Nigel Downer 26bc, Eye Of Science 67cra, /Peter Menzel 64b; Walter Myers 42–43c, Natural History Museum, London 33br, Tony Wu / Nature Picture Library 35cr, / Philippe Plailly 68t; /Philippe Plailly/Eurelios 69tc, 69cr; Millard H. Sharp 6clb, John Sibbick 47crb, Sheila Terry 47cra; **Shutterstock.com:** Mark Brandon 26–27t, Shawn Thew / EPA-EFE 69cla, Dotted Yeti 53cr; **Paul D. Taylor** 31l; **Geerat Vermeij:** Janice Fong 26bl; **Lisa D. White:** Used with permission from Lisa D. White, 24 May 2023. 63cr; **Rachel Wood:** 30bc; **University Museum of Zoology, Cambridge:** 69b; /Sarah Finney (GLAHM 100815) 65tc.

Illustrations by: John Woodcock, Eugene Fleury

Original picture research by: Kathy Lockley

All other images © Dorling Kindersley